SACRED SITES

"This symphonic epic in verse repatriates the four-billion-year history of Southern California to its native heart and soul. . . . Here is an ambitious master myth of the grand vintage we thought went out with Charles Olson and Walt Whitman. After sailing through this triumph of literary montage the Southland will never seem the same—it has become Indian Country again."

—Peter Nabokov, professor of world arts and cultures at the University of California at Los Angeles and author of *Where the Lightning Strikes: The Lives of American Indian Sacred Places*

"Suntree tells the story that is least often told, and for that alone readers can be grateful."

—Brett Garcia Myhren, *Western American Literature*

"*Sacred Sites* honors the power and beauty of our indigenous heritage and homeland. By knowing our history, we better understand the present and our journey into the future."

—Anthony Morales, tribal chair, Gabrielino Tongva Council of San Gabriel

"I simply cannot express adequately my appreciation for *Sacred Sites: The Secret History of Southern California*. It is wonderful! So full of beauty and knowledge."

—Glen MacDonald, UCLA Distinguished Professor and John Muir Memorial Chair of Geography

"A geological and cultural human history of Southern California in verse? Impossible, right? Not so, as this is exactly what California-born Susan Suntree has done. And to Suntree's credit, her performance of this 'impossible' feat is not only competent, it shines."

—Thomas Crowe, *Bloomsbury Review*

"Written in the free-verse style of field composition, this text offers itself as both an archaic and modernist scripture for a scientific era, in which 'dark energy' shapes the ephemeral and permanent natural entities—the oceans, fields, mountains, and rivers—that flash across the reader's eyes in dissociated leaps. The virtual absence of a self-referential speaker . . . makes this bardic chronicle sound more postmodern—informational, data-rich, a better fit for a generation seeking alternatives to the poetics of personal reference."

—Laurence Goldstein, in *Poetry Los Angeles: Reading the Essential Poems of the City*

"Meticulously researched geology, geography, history, and oral traditions are put in motion by a performer's touch. . . . *Sacred Sites* is an outstanding literary work, combining science with the spirituality of Native oral traditions."

—Jurgita Antoine, *Tribal College Journal*

"*Sacred Sites* is a glowing monument to the magic that trails behind each one of us humans, a sweet testament to imagination and whatever God we may acknowledge. I have nothing but respect and awe for this absolutely unique work of art."

—Carolyn See, author of *Making a Literary Life: Advice for Writers and Other Dreamers*

"Susan Suntree presents a readable and broadly accessible account of the history of the universe, Earth, and Southern California in this scholarly and creative blend of ancient myth and modern science."

—Raymond V. Ingersoll, professor of geology at the University of California, Los Angeles

"Susan Suntree demonstrates her love for the natural world along with her deep respect for the First Peoples of Southern California. The cultures of the Tongva and the Acjachemen are rich beyond measure and well documented in stories and traditions. We are not gone. We still exist. The wisdom and responsibility of being of the land is not taken lightly. Suntree appreciates and supports this connection. Years of research and writing are shared with the reader."

—Rhonda Robles, member of the Acjachemen Nation

SACRED
SITES

The Secret History of
Southern California

SUSAN SUNTREE

Foreword by Gary Snyder
Introduction by Lowell John Bean
Photographs by Juergen Nogai

University of Nebraska Press | Lincoln

All photographs © Juergen Nogai.

Library of Congress Cataloging-in-Publication Data
Suntree, Susan.
Sacred sites : the secret history of southern
California / Susan Suntree; foreword by
Gary Snyder; introduction by Lowell John Bean;
photographs by Juergen Nogai.
p. cm.
Includes bibliographical references.
ISBN 978-0-8032-3198-6 (cloth: alk. paper)
ISBN 978-1-4962-1955-8 (paperback)
1. Cosmology—Poetry. 2. Natural history—
North America—Poetry. 3. Indians of North
America—Poetry. 4. Indian mythology—California,
Southern—Poetry. 5. California, Southern—
History—Poetry. I. Title.
PS3569.U66S23 2010   811'.54—dc22   2010011310

Set in Monotype Dante by Shirley Thornton.
Designed by A. Shahan.

For the Ancestors
and
for my children,
Sean and Califia

Contents

Illustrations

Foreword GARY SNYDER

A work of great spirit accomplished with patience and vision, Susan Suntree's epic poem is a lovely weaving of science and myth. It is a work that sings. Like all good stories it reads like the storyteller is right there, speaking to the reader, shaping the universe one song at a time.

Suntree's book is about impermanence. From the very beginning, the landscape known as Southern California has reshaped itself dramatically and often. Learning how a place comes into being acquaints us with forces of life that are large and intimately interconnected. For the indigenous people, the creation and transformation of the world is an account of the First People. In this way of looking at it, the land is alive and working out its own story.

Conditions are always changing. Something always upsets the balance. Suntree recounts a pivotal moment in one of the creation myths when Frog Woman and her cronies curse the great leader Wiyot, bringing death into the world. The First People respond by sitting together and talking things over until they find ways to accommodate changed conditions and rebalance the world. The common good is at stake. Everybody participates: trees, animals, weather, and eventually the human beings. So this is a book about maintaining balance. We can only do this by carefully listening to our non-human neighbors and relatives.

But people resist letting the world in. We tend to think of the natural, the sacred, the wild as happening outside our neighborhoods and far away. Suntree brings us home. Every day in Los Angeles, tectonic plates, weather blown in from thousands of miles away, and the work of Raven and Coyote are always at play. Don't miss it!

Suntree's many years of writing, performing, and activism inform her work. So it is in part her cumulative wisdom and insight that makes this book so strong. Here we have a model for a much larger project: indigenous and Western poets and scientists swapping stories, singing their best songs around the same fire, working hard to keep the world in balance. This is going to take every song we've got.

The unique format of this extraordinary book inspired me to write its introduction. Here the reader will find scientific information presented in a way that is designed to be congruent with the Native style of oral narration and gives both perspectives in a highly readable form. Susan Suntree offers a remarkable initiation to traditional southern California philosophy. In doing so she provides an opportunity for readers not familiar with the region's cultures and geography to better understand the power of the interrelationship they have in shaping human societies.

Suntree's extensive review of ethnographic and archaeological research has allowed her to present myths and songs of the region's native people that previously have been available primarily to scholars. Her careful review of Constance Goddard DuBois's papers is particularly rewarding. In myths and especially in songs (in the case of Southern California) are found the philosophical foundations of a culture. As DuBois knew, without them we can't really understand either individual behavior or social organization.

If a culture's myths seem cryptic or abbreviated, it is because they contain codes of meaning and refer to a base of knowledge and experience not available to outsiders. For example, Western scientific explanations make sense to members of Western societies because they express commonly held assumptions. Thus, using my own expertise in and knowledge about Southern California's Native American cultures, I would like to offer a regional and ethnographic context for the data of this book. It is my hope that doing so will assist in understanding Suntree's work and also stimulate broad interest in the region's extraordinary cultural history.

The native people of Southern California developed one of the world's most complex cultures among groups who practiced hunting and gathering or had a proto-agricultural base. There was great cultural diversity because of the region's ecological features—sea coast, tidelands, rivers, mountains, foothills, lakes, and valleys. Within each of these are specific environmental niches that provided advantages and disadvantages to the people who occupied them. Additionally, the region supports two linguistic-historic traditions: the Hokan and the Takic branch of the Uto-Azetcan family of languages. This rich mixture supported a long and stable cultural history.

SETTLEMENT

The territory occupied by Southern California Indians—the Cahullia, Serrano, Luiseño, Juaneño, Tongva, Kitanimuk, Chemehuevi, Chumash—was divided unevenly into distinct geopolitical areas, each area claimed in perpetuity by a group, a lineage, or a clan. (The Kumayaay, in the San Diego area, are not described in this book.) Hundreds of communities, varying in population of fewer than one hundred to one thousand or more, were settled year round in areas that took maximum advantage of basic resources such as water (springs, streams, standing water, and the ocean) and subsistence materials. When hostile neighbors presented problems, settlements were often located in places not easily seen from a distance. Many settlements were naturally protected by virtue of being placed in narrow areas at the heads of canyons, which could be guarded fairly easily against sudden attack.

Communities were more or less permanent, with some changes in residence occurring when an individual died or was ill or when the size of a couple's family increased and necessitated more or new houses. From these communities a portion of the people would leave seasonally to collect food and other materials that were necessary for a comfortable living and, for social or ritual occasions, to visit the communities of neighboring groups.

The disparate parts of a community's landscape were connected by a complicated and well-defined trail system that made movement from area to area relatively easy. These carefully maintained trails also connected the communities to gathering, hunting, and religious sites. It was essential for everyone to know not only the differences between the trails but also all the unique identifying trail markers, in order to avoid trespassing onto land belonging to other families or privately owned land, such as shamans' power sites. Nevertheless, people from different groups often exchanged assets from their overabundance. In areas somewhat erratically useful, or in the case of game that might travel across tribal territories, neighboring groups sometimes shared access to them, such as when hunting pronghorn or gathering piñon nuts.

Throughout the territories, numerous named places could be used for various purposes because of the presence of water, food, or natural shelter. Each place was given a name, and its precise location was well memorized. Others locales were considered private and thus restricted to specific individuals because of ritual or sacred connotations. Such areas—frequently marked by petroglyphs, pictographs, and rock piles—were known to be private or dangerous because of the presence of powerful beings. Shamans and other ritual leaders frequently had sites of this kind, such as rock art sites and caves, for their own exclusive use, where they carried on esoteric activities or cached sacred materials such as the ceremonial bundle. Other places of special interest in a community included cremation areas. It is especially interesting to note that of the hundreds of place names known, many are named after a particular resource: a plant gathered there, a rock located there, a hill mentioned in oral history accounts, a place of origin, and the like.

THE COMMUNITY

The arrangement of buildings within a community was determined by ecological factors: water and food sources, shelter, and a desire for privacy. Communities often developed near springs or along streams—with the buildings generally extending along both banks—and coastal strands and estuaries. People took care to build their homes where they would not be washed away in floods, blown down by the wind, or overheated by the sun. In addition to house structures, caves and rock shelters were sometimes used for living quarters or storage, with brush shelters added in front to make the area more commodious.

Hot springs, found across Southern California as a result of the tectonic activity there, were almost invariably the focal points of the communities where they existed. In winter the hot springs environs were comparatively warm and comfortable and the waters were a pleasant way to get warm, to bathe, or to wash clothes. For those with aching bones and muscles, the springs were especially soothing, and for any sick person they were considered to have curative powers. Hot springs were places of power, both sacred and sentient, just as ordinary springs were. Southern California peoples have many recollections of unusual phenomena involving springs. Francisco Patencio wrote that people were at one time afraid of Sec he, the hot spring around which the present-day city of Palm Springs has grown up.

Various spiritual and magical personages lived in springs and could take on different forms, such as "water babies" and snakes. These and shamans could travel via a spring's extensive underground channels in order to move rapidly from one place to another. The spiritual beings associated with water existed from the beginning of creation and were personages from whom power and knowledge could be derived for healing, divination, and other magico-power activities. For these reasons the ceremonial house, quite literally the heart of any community, was placed close to the spring.

The residences of priestly extended families surrounded these central areas, in effect owning them or being responsible for the proper care of the sacred center and the religious regalia of the group. Other community members would be scattered in a somewhat isolated manner to locales west, north, and south of the central area, depending on what spots were best with respect to the sun and wind, access to useful vegetation, defense, and the location of other water resources. It was generally assumed that extended families would live together as a unit. A father and mother, their children and grandchildren, and the father's father would live together, although larger groups did sometimes cluster. Extended families would live at some distance from other extended families. Occasionally individuals, for one reason or another, would live alone and at some distance from others.

SOCIAL ORGANIZATION

Southern California Indians self-identified as belonging to a group who spoke the same language and recognized a commonly shared cultural heritage. There is no indication that these language groups ever combined for any activities as a single unit prior to European contact, although some confederation did take place shortly after contact when they united to attack or defend themselves from outsiders.

Most language groups were divided into two groups, or moieties: the *tuktum* (Wildcats) and the *'istam* (Coyotes); the Luiseño and the Chumash were exceptions.[1] Each person was a member of the moiety of his or her father, and although the moiety had no territorial boundaries, it was a very real social instrument that established ethnic identity, regulated marriages, and guided ritual reciprocity. Exogamous marriage rules at the moiety level were strict, and were maintained until recent times by some families, although they had been broken down considerably in some groups by the time W. D. Strong visited Southern California in 1924–1925. These kin groups referred to one another using names that implied family relationship and obligation and recognized common descent. The moieties served an economic and ceremonial function at most religious affairs. Intermoiety cooperation was necessary because certain components of ritual activity were owned by each moiety and these had to be integrated to complete the performance. No doubt rules that mandated this group interaction and distribution of resources were created. The requirements of marriage and ritual, along with moiety reciprocity, brought groups together at different places on a frequent basis throughout the year and also set a framework for alliances that required social and economic interaction over a long period of time.

The moiety concept was established in the beginning, when the components of the universe were each classified into one of two mutually exclusive groupings: Wildcat and Coyote, beings associated with the Creators who dichotomized the cosmological realm.[2] The consequences of this separation were immediately related to ecological-subsistence needs. Within the territories of either moiety, significantly different ecological patterns made for varying deficiencies of needed resources at any given time, and thus the system required an exchange of goods and some sharing of goods and services.

THE CEREMONIAL BUNDLE

Each independent group had a ceremonial bundle initially created by the first religious leader in its history. The reeds from which the wrappings were made were acquired at the ocean in the early time of creation by Coyote, who served as the first ceremonial leader. Thus the sacredness of the bundle and its contents was rooted in tradition. This was the most important set of objects in Indian life among the Southern California peoples.

The ceremonial bundle was a reed mat that was four or five feet in width and fifteen to twenty feet in length; it enclosed ceremonial objects such as feather ropes, shell beads used in ceremonial exchange, bone whistles, curved sticks, tobacco, and other ritual items. Within the bundle a supernatural power suggestive of the Creator that communicated with the religious leader existed; the religious leader regularly addressed this power using an esoteric language and regularly fed it native tobacco.

The ceremonial bundle and its equivalents served as a symbolic representation of each group. The bundle validated life: reli-

gious, political, social, and economic. As a sacred object the bundle connected the people with the "beginning," the time when all the good things of life came, when food was created, when ceremonial and political structures were given to the people, and when they first occupied their territories and received the songs they sang.

The adjudicative and administrative roles of the religious and political leaders were supported by the ceremonial bundle and other ritual objects since they could call upon the bundle's power as a sanctioning device to punish illegal behavior. The bundle was integral to the economy as well. Its power was used when the community performed its annual rites of increase, and its possession reaffirmed the right of the people to live in the land whose resources they exploited. It was used to control positions of hereditary leaders and those who had achieved high status and recognition by their use of supernatural power.

THE LEADERS

The community leader, sometimes called the captain or chief by English speakers, managed the people in many ways. He was responsible for the correct maintenance of ritual and the care and maintenance of the ceremonial bundle and the ceremonial house. The ritual activity kept the environment in proper balance.

The community leader served as economic manager, determining where and when people would go to gather foods or hunt game. He knew, having been advised by those who knew, where the food-gathering places were located and would instruct people when to gather. He also had the privilege of first gathering if he so chose. The food he gathered would be eaten at the ceremonial house.

The leader administered first-fruit rites prior to the gathering of acorns, mesquite, and other staples, and he collected goods that he either stored for future ceremonial use, exchanged with other groups, or used for emergency rations. He was responsible for remembering group boundaries and individual ownership rights so that when conflict arose between individual families or within lineages or clans, he could adjudicate them.

Significant political roles were also ascribed to the leader's assistant, to the singers, and to the shamans. When there was an important political decision to be made, they met with the leader. When an important man in the community was to be censured, or a legal dispute arose that had repercussions beyond an individual or family level, these men were called upon for their opinions and support. They also acted to punish offenders on behalf of the lineages.

THE LEADER'S ASSISTANT

The leader's assistant provided ceremonial, administrative, and adjudicating support. He was an integral part of all rites, ceremonies, and functions (birth, puberty, first-fruit, death, and others), and no other person could assume his specifically defined duties or roles of his office (which tended to be based on hereditary). The assistant participated fully in the economic phases of community life by organizing and leading certain community hunting and gathering activities (usually ceremonially instigated), and by gathering and distributing the food throughout the community as needed.

He was a man who inspired respect and fear among the people and was obeyed without question. His power was justified by tradition, as it was Coyote who served as the first assistant at the first funeral ceremonies for Mukat (Cahuilla) or Wiyot (Luiseño, Juaneño, Gabrielino).

RELIGIOUS DANCERS AND SINGERS

The person who knew sacred music and dances and who led their performance played a role in each of these groups. Dancing, which was integral to most ritual performances among Takic- and Hokan-speaking peoples, portrayed dramatic persons and events in the groups' histories and cosmologies. Dance performances were complex events that ranged from the swift, elegantly performed eagle dance (simulating an eagle's flight) to ponderously careful and dramatically significant war dances to emotionally meaningful dances associated with burying images of the dead. Dances and dancing required choreographic talent, stamina, and a sense of mimicry, rhythm, timing, and imagination.

SHAMANS

Shamans formed an elite group, acting together with the tribal leader and the leader's assistant to express opinions, make decisions, and provide offerings to the Sacred Bundle, especially in times of disaster and epidemic. Shamans often met in the sweathouse, using it as a sort of "club-house." The tribal leaders were usually shamans and therefore controlled the political structure by weaving it into a tightly interacting group who increased its power over the communities. Thus, an association of shamans cut across clan and lineage boundaries to form an association of power-oriented persons. On occasion shamans demonstrated control of power by public fire-eating and sword-swallowing demonstrations.

Possession of supernatural power was necessary for becoming a member of the powerful and somewhat secret society of shamans. This power was acquired by one of several means: an individual could be born with it, it could be passed from another shaman, or it could be received from a spirit being.

The economic activities of these men were critical to a successful life for the community. They were able to "create" food.

When there was a scarcity of food or when there was a prediction of scarcity, they brought forth a miniature food-producing tree such as an oak from their hands during a public performance, thereby magically ensuring that the season's acorn crop would be plentiful. This act has been described by Cahuilla elder Victoria Las Wierick:

> When the "witch man" made acorn trees in his palm, he got hot coals in his hands and he held it there and it came like a weed growing in the ground. It grew that high [about two inches]—this would make food come when there was no food. There are none of them that way anymore.[3]

The treatment of some diseases was another responsibility of the shamans. These included not only the medical problems that occurred naturally—such as wounds, snakebites, and accidents—but also those caused by an attack from another shaman, supernatural punishment for the infraction of rituals and taboos, soul loss, and malevolency of spirits prior to a death ceremony. The shaman was also responsible for ensuring that an individual thought to be dead was not simply in a trancelike state. Shamans cured diseases by sucking diseased objects from the patient's body or blowing to send away evil, as well as using various medically useful herbs and minerals, exercise, and procedures such as setting fractured bones. These acts were accompanied by songs and natural methods, including the use of herbs and massage.

The shaman was also a diviner who understood signs given by birds, animals, and celestial bodies. He could predict such things as impending illness or certain death. He knew, for instance, that a soul was lost when he saw a falling star, and could proceed to discover whose soul it was and return it to the person before one of several soul-catching beings found it. He also could see impending disaster—flood, drought, famine, or epidemic—which required gathering together the people and taking action to offset malevolent spirits. By utilizing the combined powers of the shamans and the ceremonial bundle, disasters were sometimes averted.

THE CURER

In sharp contrast to these other personages there was also a curer who utilized no supernatural power. A curer was often a woman who learned her medical lore from other curers. There were no formal installations in this role, as a person usually learned gradually through experience and through time became known and trusted in the community for his or her skill. Most curers were middle-aged or older, and they possessed great knowledge concerning medical herbs, the specifics for various conditions such as childbirth, and ailments such as wounds, broken bones, or intestinal discomfort.

The curer role was economically advantageous. The practitioner was customarily paid for his or her services in food, baskets, or other goods. If the curer did not know how to cure a disease, he or she called upon the services of the shaman. There are accounts, however, of a shaman assigning a curer to carry out his medical instructions for a patient who might require the service for many days. It is reported that curers were sometimes suspected of using magical power "to achieve personal ends."

The people of Southern California were stable and settled for many thousands of years before European contact. Political stability was supported in large part because of the complex system of economic exchanges that crossed sociopolitical and cultural boundaries. Sophisticated technologies for exploiting the region's variety of food sources also contributed to the region's stability. These advantages were enhanced by the social institutions of marriage and ritual whose requisite exchanges interlocked peoples living in different environments and resulted in a regular flow of goods from one group to another. The combination of a fortunate environment, generations of adaptation, and the invention of ecologically adaptive social structures allowed the native people to thrive for millennia.

NOTES

1. While indications suggestive of moiety structure among the Luiseños were observed by William Duncan Strong, he could find no evidence of a functioning moiety system in place. Strong, *Aboriginal Society in Southern California*, 288. The record of Chumash social structure, which was apparently similar to that of the more northerly groups such as the Pomo, is too scant to define as "moiety structured."

2. In the respective creation accounts, the Cahuilla Mukat and Temayawut, who are brother creators, are roughly equivalent to the Serrano creator brothers, Pakrikitat and Kukitat. But the Luiseño Táukumit and Tamáayawut are respectively male and female creators, the parents of Wiyot. Strong has discussed similarities and differences between Cahuilla, Cupeño, and Luiseño creation stories. *Aboriginal Society in Southern California*, 325.

3. Personal communication.

Book One, "Western Science," is presented chronologically and dates are meant to
be seen as bookends between which many
events unfold. Mythic time is another matter. It can be imagined as a pool where all
time is present at once.

The texts of both "Western Science" and
Book Two, "Myths and Songs," are presented as lines to encourage readers to hear
them as though they are listening to a
storyteller or singer. In Southern California,
when the ancient creation myths were performed (as they still are among people who
practice the original ways), they were often interspersed with personal songs, which
lent an individual and emotional tone to
the cosmological themes of the creation
stories. In "Myths and Songs" these personal songs are set off visually from the main
text.

My versions of the myths and songs
in Book Two are based primarily on the
records of ethnographers who usually
worked with tribal translators. Many of
these documents were recorded as prose or
word-for-word transliterations. Since the
recitation of myths and songs was always
a component of rituals and ceremonies, I
have attempted to express their qualities
of oral performance and poetry. Though
repetition of lines and words is a common
feature of the performance of myths and
songs, I have omitted much of the repetition in order to focus on the core of each
piece.

Book Two begins with a Quechnajuichom (Luiseño) creation myth based
on the recitation by Lucario Cuevish to
Constance Goddard DuBois in 1908. The
myths and songs of Southern California
share common characters and themes,
though these differ in the telling from family to family, tribe to tribe, and geographic
area to geographic area. For example, there
are distinct differences between the versions told by groups living near the coast
and those living near the mountains. Using Cuevish's recitation as a base, I weave
in other ways of recounting the creation,
which suggests the myths' multiplicity
of interpretations and ways of being told
(rather than there being only one holy text).
Similarly, narrative plots evolve by branch-
ing from a core that is well known to the
original listeners. More information about
my sources and how certain myths were
originally performed is found in the notes.

I usually don't name tribes but instead
provide a readily identifiable landmark
where each tribe is centered. An overview
of tribal boundaries is illustrated on the
map as well. Also, early twentieth-century
ethnographers recorded the Spanish word
meaning "captain" for what we now call
"chief," and the word "doctor" for "shaman." I have continued this practice.

Southern California has long been a
homeland. Even Wilshire Boulevard is a
very old trail traveled for millennia. My
hope is that understanding the deep character and cultural beauty of the region will
open our collective eyes and influence the

ways we live here. Writing this book has changed me. The landscape no longer ends with the concrete. Layers of life beckon from the expanse of the basin and the rise of hills and mountains.

Of course, in a work of this nature there is plenty of mystery to go around. Conclusions taken as fact today eventually will be revised or transformed. Myths also evolve because their recitation is inflected to a region and to an era when they are told. And each performer brings to bear on the text his or her unique talents and insights. This plasticity of science, myths, and songs reminds me that it's all alive, all changing, always.

SACRED SITES

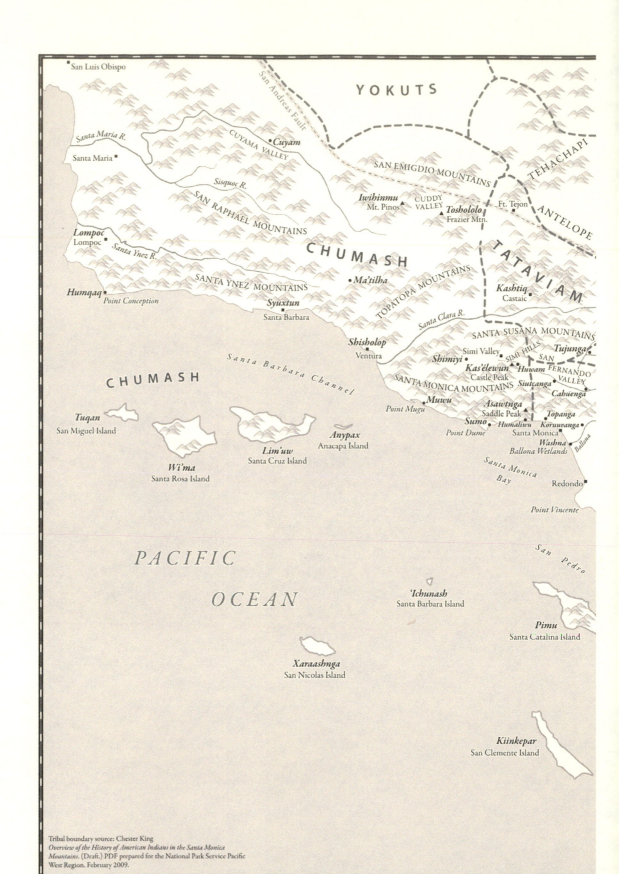

- San Luis Obispo

YOKUTS

San Andreas Fault

Santa Maria R.

CUYAMA VALLEY

• **Cuyam**

- Santa Maria

SAN EMIGDIO MOUNTAINS

TEHACHAPI

Sisquoc R.

SAN RAPHAEL MOUNTAINS

Iwihinmu
Mt. Pinos

CUDDY VALLEY

• Ft. Tejon

Toshololo
Frazier Mtn.

ANTELOPE

Lompoc
Lompoc

Santa Ynez R.

CHUMASH

TATAVIAM

SANTA YNEZ MOUNTAINS

• **Ma'tilha**

TOPATOPA MOUNTAINS

Kashtiq
Castaic

Humqaq
Point Conception

Syuxtun
Santa Barbara

Santa Clara R.

SANTA SUSANA MOUNTAINS

Shisholop
Ventura

Shimiyi
Simi Valley

SIMI HILLS

Tujunga

SAN FERNANDO VALLEY

CHUMASH

Santa Barbara Channel

Kas'elewun
Castle Peak

Huwam

Siutcanga

Cahuenga

Muwu

SANTA MONICA MOUNTAINS

Point Mugu

Asawtnga
Saddle Peak

Topanga

Tuqan
San Miguel Island

Sumo

Humaliwu

Koruuvanga

Anypax
Anacapa Island

Point Dume

Santa Monica

Washna
Ballona Wetlands

Ballona

Lim'uw
Santa Cruz Island

Wi'ma
Santa Rosa Island

Santa Monica Bay

Redondo

Point Vincente

San Pedro

PACIFIC

OCEAN

'Ichunash
Santa Barbara Island

Pimu
Santa Catalina Island

Xaraashnga
San Nicolas Island

Kiinkepar
San Clemente Island

Tribal boundary source: Chester King
Overview of the History of American Indians in the Santa Monica
Mountains. (Draft.) PDF prepared for the National Park Service Pacific
West Region. February 2009.

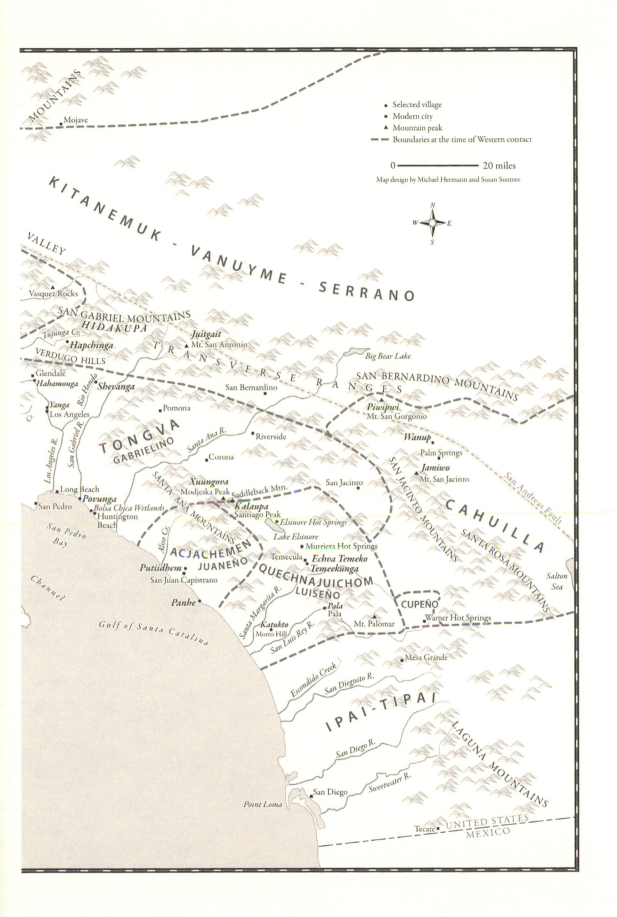

MOUNTAINS

Mojave

- Selected village
■ Modern city
▲ Mountain peak
--- Boundaries at the time of Western contact

0 ——————— 20 miles

Map design by Michael Hermann and Susan Suntree

N
W E
S

KITANEMUK - VANUYME - SERRANO

VALLEY

Vasquez Rocks

SAN GABRIEL MOUNTAINS
HIDAKUPA

Tujunga Cr.

Hapchinga

Juitgait
▲ Mt. San Antonio

Big Bear Lake

TRANSVERSE RANGES

VERDUGO HILLS

Glendale

Hahamonga

San Bernardino

SAN BERNARDINO MOUNTAINS

Rio Hondo

Shevanga

Pomona

Yanga
Los Angeles

Piwipwi
▲ Mt. San Gorgonio

San Gabriel R.

TONGVA
GABRIELINO

Santa Ana R.

Riverside

Wanup
■ Palm Springs

Los Angeles R.

Corona

Jamiwo
▲ Mt. San Jacinto

San Andreas Fault

Long Beach

Xuungova
Modjeska Peak ▲

Saddleback Mtn.

San Jacinto

SAN JACINTO MOUNTAINS

CAHUILLA

San Pedro

Povunga

SANTA ANA MOUNTAINS

Kalaupa
Santiago Peak

SANTA ROSA MOUNTAINS

Bolsa Chica Wetlands
Huntington
Beach

Aliso Cr.

Elsinore Hot Springs

Lake Elsinore

Salton
Sea

San Pedro
Bay

ACJACHEMEN
JUANEÑO

Murrieta Hot Springs

Temecula

Echva Temeko
Temeekúnga

Channel

Putiidhem
San Juan Capistrano

QUECHNAJUICHOM
LUISEÑO

CUPEÑO

Panhe

Santa Margarita R.

Pala
Pala

Warner Hot Springs

Gulf of Santa Catalina

Katukto
Morro Hill

San Luis Rey R.

▲ Mt. Palomar

■ Mesa Grande

Escondido Creek

San Dieguito R.

IPAI-TIPAI

LAGUNA MOUNTAINS

San Diego R.

Sweetwater R.

San Diego

Point Loma

Tecate

UNITED STATES
MEXICO

Book One ❦ WESTERN SCIENCE

1   *Light, Space, Matter*

In the beginning
                        unutterable
                                        hot
                                                no space
        no time

                (not shape not size not taste not smell not see not touch)

                                a singular nothing
nothing-at-all
        compressed to a point, infinitely dense
                                        wobbling

14 BILLION YEARS AGO
Colossal balloom!
                The Big Bang
                                        seething radiation
        no center no edge

roiling gaseous universe soup
                pure energy pops riotous sparks
                        (or the spectral harmonics of minute energy strings)
                wild infinitesimal bits: the six quarks:
                                up down strange charmed truth beauty
                        the three leptons (electron, muon, tauon) and
                        the little neutral ones: neutrinos
                whirl in and out of colliding light
        particle annihilating antiparticle
                blasting photons at every turn—
                                the first frenzied pips
                                        radiate forever into unfathomable mystery
                (What caused it? Came before it?
                Into what belly, what field did it blast?)
        energy to mass
                mass to energy
                        plasma pounding to particles and back to wave

gravity overcome by the speeding inflation
                              and walloping heat.

The Big Bang births space
                                        as it expands
                        time as it travels
doubling its size in seconds.

Shock waves throb through the plasma,
                        ringing the cosmos like a temple bell.

Temperature falling—the hot whirling
                              slightly cools:
Three quarks cling to each other (up up down)
                              and settle as protons: positive charge
Three quarks cling to each other (down down up)
                              and settle as neutrons: no charge,
Electrons settle: negative charge.

                              Forms ripen in nothing's singular field

The same proton, neutron, electron
                        throughout space-time
                              (star, tongue, tear, plastic fork)

                        Our bodies as old as the cosmos.

Colliding, cooking, particles fuse into nuclei—
            the seed at the center of atoms:
                        a single proton we name hydrogen
                  one proton plus one neutron: deuterium.
                        When two deuterium, bang together and bond: helium
                        In the hot frenzy,
                                    almost all the deuterium in the whole universe
                  transforms into helium (two protons)

The birth of matter!
            Hydrogen (seventy-five percent of the visible universe)
            and a little Helium (twenty-five percent).

Space-time, porous and strange,
spreads out in all directions—
            an etheric fabric stretching itself
                    against the attractions of gravity
        it hovers
                in the movement of matter.

                        (Gravity, the busy mystery: What is it?
                The curve in the bed—space-time—when we—matter/energy—sit?
                The dander—weightless infinite pushy particles—
                        shed from every dog in the universe?)

Invisible, baffling   Dark Matter
                (no light burning nor mirrored, no light at all)
                in gravity-collected clouds it dark-halos the visible:
                protons, neutrons, electrons

                        (and will holdfast from flying apart
                        the coming galaxies)

Invisible, baffling   Dark Energy
                gravity repelling, stretching, flattening
                innate to the fabric of space-time

Ninety-six percent of this story, of everything: Dark
        (our elegant theories!)
                        veiled, impervious, mute.

Expanding and cooling   Expanding and cooling   Expanding and cooling

        Light takes off

                                spreading through space-time
But matter congeals
Electrons, hovering in layers, cling to the nuclei
        (one electron per proton):

hydrogen and helium (become)

                                    atoms.

The electrons absorb photons from the vast light swarm
Energized, electrons jump from rung to rung, hot-footing
up an energy ladder away from the nucleus
until, tottering at the top, they jump
to fly loose and alluring into space
or to the arms of another atom
or, insistent on being shared, wed atoms into molecules.
If, tiring of adventure, they climb
back down the ladder toward the nucleus
they release their stash of photons
that rush away glowing (light and heat).

(We chase after rowdy electrons,
whose swapping and
sharing charges / changes
everything we measure.
We call it chemistry.)

And so the future of the universe
formed at its birth:
(All the energy that will ever be was born at the beginning).

Teeter-tottering between
visible / invisible motion and visible / invisible matter

Collapse
to another (the same?)
primordial infinite point
(Big Bang reversed)

or

Infinite expansion:
ceaselessly stretching space-time
(stars like boats sailing on an ever-widening sea)

or

Infinite expansion
      ceaselessly shredding space-time
            (galaxies, planets, bird wings, atoms torn to bits)

or

Perfect balance
      gravity (motion) and mass (Dark Matter) in perfect balance
         (and it all stands still).

Gravity pulls hydrogen atoms
          into massive cooling gaseous clouds.
More mass means more gravity.
      Hydrogen clouds contract.
             Friction!
Temperatures rising
      atoms stirred up
Hydrogen atoms, bounced around,
        lose their electrons that billow into
Plasma clouds: loose protons and electrons
    leap and spin
      in gravity's blender

hotter and hotter
tighter and tighter
closer and closer.

In the cloud's seething shrinking center
    protons melt together
        and melt together again and again:
hydrogen into deuterium into helium.

Copious radiation from the fusions
flows forth as
      starlight.

The largest stars
            pull themselves together
            hotter, harder than all the others

Bigger the star, faster the burn.
Life as short as ten million years.

As hydrogen fuses into helium
            the core of a giant star
            grows heavier
Gravity holds down the lid
            and the temperature heats up.

The inferno bakes new atoms:
            Take one proton: hydrogen (H)
                        Attach one neutron to hydrogen: deuterium (D)
                        Mix two deuterium: helium (He2)
                        Mix two helium—(He2) plus (He2): beryllium (Be4)
                        Mix one beryllium (Be4) with one more helium (He2): carbon (C6)

            From one proton: carbon
                        the staff of life on Earth.

2   *Galaxy, Planet, Moon, Rain*

Cooking and consuming itself
growing its own gravity
elements into new elements
      waves of radiation released with every bite
        hotter and denser
    the star grows heavier   heavier and heavier

        carbon silicon gold calcium iron

all the atoms of rock and flesh
forged inside the doomed star
           (alchemy in the stellar kitchen).

Small and medium-sized stars
digest their hydrogen (protons)
          more slowly
cook only into helium
    that wafts away in gaseous layers
abandoning its electrons to compact in shrunken cores
      hot dry old bones: White Dwarfs
           scattered across the universe.

When massive stars
    burn out
   (hydrogen ripened into heavy elements—
           a seed pod ready to burst)
   less and less heat
      resists
        gravity's hand.

Collapse!
Explosion!   Super Nova! (Super New)
   blasting into space
   stellar ash
   rich with the new elements

A cosmic compost ready
                              for new gardens.

The gardener, gravity,
                    rakes new elemental clouds into fresh stars
                              what's left over into hedgerows:
                                        planets, moons, and meteors.

And so all the elements,
              cycle in and out of stars
              round and round and round.

The burst large star's
                    old core
                    shrunk to a tiny
                    massively heavy, radiating, rotating lump:
                                                  Neutron Star.

But when gigantic stars with serious mass
                    (born from colossal hydrogen clouds)
                    burn out,
Catastrophic collapse
            unstoppable gravity
                              heats and withers the core
Not even light escapes

                    space-time stops

Black Hole.

Gravity: Eros and appetite
weaves dust into massive hydrogen whorls haloed by dark matter
where clutches of stars form in luminous nests:
                                        galaxies
                                        like spinning elliptical lozenges
                                        or whirling discs with spiral arms.

Gravity
       feeds one galaxy to another and they fatten
       gathers galaxies
             into neighborhoods.

Ours is the Local Group,
          thirty galaxies hung together
          traveling together across the web of space-time.

More than two trillion galaxies in the universe.

10 BILLION YEARS AGO
Orbiting the Local Group
            a spiral galaxy, by mammals named: The Milky Way
               (a top, a flying saucer, a whirling white rose)
                  more than 100 billion stars.

The first stars form in its bulging center.

New stars,
       gathered from elements
           burst from the first stars
       blaze in its vast feathery arms
                  Orion
                  Sagittarius
                  Perseus
                  Centaurus
                  Cygnus

And all together they revolve,
       slowly clockwise
       around the galactic center's
           great Black Hole.

4.5 BILLION YEARS AGO
Turning slowly
       on the inner edge of Orion's Arm

A giant gas cloud: hydrogen, a little helium,
        and a dust of star-baked heavy elements
  collapses   sharp, tight
     into a spinning disk
        heavy elements swing to the edge
        as the cloud swirls inward upon itself.

At the center, atom dissolving storms
    fuse nuclei: hydrogen into deuterium into helium

In the whirling fusion furnace
A small star is born and set in orbit around the galaxy:
                  Sun.

Enough fuel to burn for ten billion years.
(We say: Five billion more to go!)

Carried within Orion's Arm, Sun circles the galaxy
    Galaxy circles the Local Group
      Local Group sails through the universe.

Temperatures fall in the spinning disc
At the sun's fringe a debris of dust, gas, heavy elements
               condenses into grains.
The grains collide
     melt
     into minerals
     minerals combine
     into rocks.

Gravity spins
     elemental gas and rocky minerals
     into planets, moons, asteroids, comets, meteors

Solar rays sweep gases
     from rocky inner planets: Mercury
                    Venus
                    Earth
                    Mars

1

Winter Solstice petroglyph: Simi Hills.

to an asteroid belt of leftovers: dust, ice, rubble, miles-wide boulders

    to outer gaseous planets: Jupiter

            Saturn

            Uranus

            Neptune

      to the Kuiper Belt of frozen rocky remnants

            and the ice dwarf planet, Pluto.

Space in the solar system clears.

Sunlight flows through the space

        heating the planets.

Inner heat softens the third planet from the sun.

Light elements bubble to the surface

Heavy elements, iron and nickel, congeal

    and sink to the center of the Earth

            as a hot, heavy core

        center of the core: solid, nearly as hot as the surface of the sun

            spinning faster than the Earth

       surface of the core: dense plastic liquid

        a roiled ocean of iron

          boiling on the core's blazing stove

      wrapped in a scalding, ever-so-slow-flowing mineral mantle:

        Oxygen, Silicon, Aluminum, Iron,

        Calcium, Sodium, Potassium, Magnesium

      which rises in volcanic blasts through cracks in the crust

       as all the world's bedrock and beach

         stones,

           pebbles,

            and sand.

The turbulent liquid surface of the core, seethed by heat

        and whirled into storms by the Earth's rotation

    stirs up a magnetic field

    a dynamo

    an Earth-magnet:

        magnetic north pole

        magnetic south pole

The poles' radiant arms form a field
        embracing the Earth
                shielding from lethal cosmic rays
                      delicate chemical arrangements
                    (the meetings and matings
                      of life forms to come).

But, now and again, about every 400–700 hundred thousand years
            the arms weaken
                    disorganize
                      (shifts in the core's hot swirling mystery?)

                      their safeguard withers, rearranges.

When they revive,
            polarities switched
                    (magnetic north to magnetic south),

                          they remain for a while
          and switch again.

And so the Earth swaps its magnetic self
                north south north south north south

In iron-rich magma,
        flowing from the mantle
                through plate cracks and fissures or steamed through volcanoes
                      onto the surface of the Earth
                      onto deep seafloor,
      iron electrons in the magma line up,
                    and as it hardens
        the compass is fixed.

The pole reversals (north south north south north south)
               pattern the crust
      with magnetic strips
                recording the epoch when each strip cooled.

Heart of the planet:

radiant

molten

magnetic.

Asteroids, comets, meteorites,
    fierce and hot,
        bombard the young planet.
            The battering keeps it spinning.
Suddenly
    a rock the size of Mars
        whacks the Earth a lateral blow,
            tilting its axis,
    and explodes itself and the Earth.

Gravity gathers the wreckage in a halo of rubble,
and slowly fashions a sphere it tethers to the restored Earth

And so the Moon cycles the Earth
    every twenty-eight days
            (tides, menses, the origins of a month).

The young planet settles,
    contracting,
        it cools

As the surface cools into crust,
    molten rocks dry and harden
    releasing water trapped in their mineral webs
Asteroids smash into the crust delivering their water
Volcanoes explode magma into ash, minerals, carbon dioxide, nitrogen, water vapor

The primeval atmosphere weaves water into clouds

The great rains begin

Extravagant rains
                              stream into oceans

Oceans of rain.

This watery rock
We name   Earth   The Blue Planet

Right here.

Rivers of rain pour over rocks carrying
                    their mineral-salts into the oceans

Sunshine evaporates ocean water into clouds
                         leaving the salts behind

As the world's water cycles
                              in and out of clouds
the oceans slowly grow salty.

3 *Wandering North America, Life, Death*

(Our dark rocky mother, newborn, besieged,
                              sweltering,
                                        circling a young sun)
Earthquakes, sulfurous stinking vapors
eruptions, bombardment, lightning, solar radiation

In the seething vat of atoms
                    hydrogen carbon nitrogen sulfur oxygen
                    share electrons, fasten into molecules in a flurry of forms
                                        we name: the amino acids

In the seething vat of atoms
                    carbon and nitrogen
                    share electrons, fasten into a molecule
                                        we name: cyanide

Sunlight powers cyanide to arrange and rearrange with hydrogen,
                    (add a sprinkle of oxygen)
                    and fashions these into five forms of tiny rings
                                        we name: the bases

                                        (basics in the primal kitchen)

Stirred in the world's shallow wet
                    water and carbon hook up as sugar
                    shed water and share electrons to
                    hook up with phosphate and the bases:
                                        concocting a brand new group of molecules

                                        we name: Ribonucleic Acid   RNA.

Sweet   poison fireworks
                    molecules move in the direction of life.

2

Springs at the village of Koruuvanga, near where Portola camped on his 1769
expedition to Monterey: University High School, West Los Angeles.

Meteors and comets pummel the planet
       seed and stir the hot, wet rock with
              more amino acids and bases arriving as molecules readymade
              more elements: hydrogen, oxygen, carbon, nitrogen, sulfur, silicon

Perhaps in pond scum or boiling deep-ocean vents,
       perhaps in the long, linear,
              crystalline layers of primordial clay
In mysterious catalytic moments
       RNA, jiggling wildly through the hot world,
          sends out small scouts of itself
            to trap loose beads of amino acid
              (one each of the twenty that fit)
         attaching the beads to itself
         tying each amino acid to the next:
                  self-assembly.

(We will name these strings: protein.)

RNA disconnects and moves away.

The new protein strings float around, fall apart,
              float around, fall apart,
                float around, fall apart.

Deep inside the loose RNA, a phosphate molecule
       yearns to exchange electrons
          with the only unattached oxygen (O!)

       but when they do it,
              the molecule splits up

              a drama repeating itself
         over and over and over,

until, one day,
       after bouncing into chemical catalysts
         over and over and over
     (matches struck and burned out; lessons learned and forgotten),

the Ribonucleic Acid
        evicts irresistible oxygen (O)

            stabilizing itself as a spiral:

De-oxy-ribo Nucleic Acid   DNA

           Deoxyribonucleic Acid:
                its body built as code so sturdy
                  it lasts through the ages.

                    The birth of memory.

           Sloshing around the hot world

DNA collects, attaching to itself
        loose bits of RNA that fit its bases
and the RNA collects, attaching to itself according to its sequence
        loose bits of amino acids
            tying the amino acids one to another:
                coded protein strings.

DNA and RNA detach and float away,
        leaving behind their protein progeny.

But one day, in an ordinary moment on Earth,
        (random mutation, selection, mystery)
           in undiscovered beds or on the skin of bubbling primal scum
      from knitted protein strings
           the first cell is born.

Life and death.

3.8 BILLION YEARS AGO
First the mysterious air-eaters:
                one-celled bacteria
          float in tropically warm waters beneath carbon dioxide skies
          churn deep underwater in hot sulfurous volcanic vents

absorbing: dissolved hydrogen (H) and carbon (C)
releasing: methane (CH_4)

Next the light-eaters:
                    blue-green bacteria
                              All day into chlorophyll's electron mouths
                                        bites of light (photons)
                    Excited, their electron bellies swell
                                   knocking apart water (H_2O)
                                   soaking up carbon dioxide (CO_2)
                         assembling a cuisine of carbohydrates (CH_2O)
                         freeing a waste of oxygen (O)
                         breathed out all night.

Iron dissolved in the worldwide oceans
          absorbs the oxygen
                    and sinks to the bottom in layers of sediment.

Minerals collect in the first grains of the (coming) land
                                   (we will someday name
                                        North America).

2.5 BILLION YEARS AGO
                    Beneath temperate seas
the crust of the busy Earth breaks
                    (into snake scales, puzzle pieces, eccentric dinner plates)
and these huge rocky plates
          float
                    on the slow streaming mantle.

One thousand eight hundred miles beneath the crust
                                        the Earth's white-hot core
                              along with the radioactive elements that are always
                    coming apart
                              radiate primeval heat
                    softening, expanding the mantle
          until its miles thick, dense mineral body
      flows up toward the surface.

Cooling as it rises, the mantle contracts
　　　　　and sinks back toward the center
　　　　　　　　　　to heat and rise again
　　　　　　　　　　　　　　　　expanding and contracting over and over
　　　　　　　　　　　　　　　　　　　　　　in slow cycles
　　　　　　　(Martha Graham, cool milk swirled by hot coffee)

　　　　　　　　　　　　　　　　　　　　　　magnificent secret wheels
　　　　　　　　cracking, heaving, carrying
　　　　　　　　the crust's giant plates.

Magma　　　mother of rock
the mantle's primal mineral mix
　　　　　hot, viscous, dark fount of all the rocks on Earth
　　　　　　　　　　　　　(prison walls, garden paths, pebble in the horse's hoof)
　　　　　gushes up
　　　　　　　　　through cracks in the crust when the plates pull apart
　　　　　filling the gaps
　　　　　　　　thickening the crust where it collects
　　　　　　　　　　　　　　　　and cools.

Some of the magma swells all the way up and spills over the surface (lava)
　　　　　　　　　　　and cools to a dense deep dark-gray rock (basalt)
Some magma, thrust deep into the old crust,
　　　　　　　　rises through the layers
　　　　　　　　　　　　　　so slowly
　　　　　　　　cools and rises
　　　　　　　　　　　　　shedding minerals as it rises,
　　　　　　　　　　　　　　　　　so slowly lightened
　　　　　　　　crystallizing as it rises to a quartz froth
　　　　　　　fermented to sparkling granite

　　　　　　buoying the crust from beneath
　　　　　　lifting land above the water:
　　　　　　　　　　　　　the first continents.

When ocean and continental plates
　　　　　converge

the continent, thicker but lighter,
                  survives by bobbing up—a cork in a bucket—
the dense dark ocean crust
        bends in a deep bow
          (a breaching whale's curved back and nose-down dive)
                under the continent

mantle-pushed and gravity-pulled under
             the ocean crust slowly flows into the hot mantle.
               Absorbed, the plate disappears.

While the two bodies rub hard together
    the feverish ocean plate
        wet with sea water and its own mineral sweat
            superheated to steam
       melts the continent's deep underside
          blasting it all
          through any fissure it finds
   building battalions of volcanoes
       inland along the continental plate's edge
        igniting a volley of farewells:
                 lava, gas, boulders, and ash
                    strewn for hundreds of miles.

Volcanoes cool off and settle,
        give over to sun, wind,
           and the rain that washes it all downstream
             to swelling river deltas.

More news of the ocean plate's journey and loss:
         rocks scraped off its back as it's swallowed
         pile up on the continental edge

and so the continents slowly fatten.

Thin and flat, the core of North America
              rises above the water.

Afloat in the old oceans

                                  or nestled in shallow bays
          some single cells embrace or invade other single cells
               and one makes itself at home

               inside the other, fattened cell.

Blue-green bacteria move inside algae and settle
               as cells of chlorophyll:
                                the algae turns green.

Some cells divide, copying themselves,
         and later, in primal egalitarian generosity (joy?)
               some cells divide, swapping DNA
                                    fifty-fifty

     Sex!

The seas grow green. Algae exhale oxygen.
Iron in the oceans absorbs some of the oxygen.

All the rest, unhindered, bubbles right through ocean waters into the air.

                    Around the water-glistening sphere
                        gases rise and cling in a vaporous blanket.
One of the sun's radiations, ultraviolet light,
                         like a can opener, cuts open water vapors:
             hydrogen   hydrogen   oxygen

             Hydrogen escapes into space
             Heavier, oxygen envelopes the Earth

From algae's breath and broken water vapor: the oxygen-rich air is born.

Oxygen rusts the iron
          in minerals exposed to the new air: red dirt.

The rivers of the world run red.

More and more and more oxygen: Oxygen Catastrophe!
Defenseless against the poisonous new air that bursts cells to bits,
    ancient bacteria must hide, change, or die.

          (Some still hide, alive and well,
             in the cow's gut
             exhaling methane
             through the cow's nose.)

Mutating, or (mysteriously) selecting, or dividing
                  every twenty minutes,
    the cell survivors
        create chemical shields against oxygen
            (antioxidents we name vitamins C and E)
        make and remake themselves, struggling
    the first cellular steps
        toward oxygen-breathing animal life.

          (We breathe
          the opposite of trees
          oxygen in, carbon dioxide out.)

Wide, rough tables of dry rock—the cratons:
          cores or kernels of the continents
          linger above and slip back below sea level
     They split and merge   split and merge
       churned by streams of magma
        roiling beneath the crust

North America: a small brown box turtle dawdling across the equator
    Its small shell like a shield:
          land we name Montana, Wyoming, Minnesota
          Ontario, Greenland, West Britain.

3

Interior, Cave of Munits: West Hills.

1.6 BILLION YEARS AGO
New bouts of magma, thick hot mush,
        propelled by heat and the lessening pressure as it rises
        steamed from chthonic depths
   burst and burn into deep loads of dirt washed to the western rim of North America
        planting the first layer of the coming mountains:
        San Gabriels, San Bernardinos
    cooking the rocks already there into new minerals
          to one day be named
             the oldest rock in Southern California,
        a glittering, layered confection: Mendenhall Gneiss.

Huge bolts of magma steam into the ancient rock fifteen miles beneath
            the sea-covered surface
                    and slowly crystallize
                            to rare, white, glittering anorthosite

    (coming white cliffs in the San Gabriel and Chocolate Mountains).

                        (The pale face of the moon is made of anorthosite.)

1 BILLION YEARS AGO

Barren rocky continents bake by day, freeze by night.

High over the Earth
        sunlight
                    welds oxygen into ozone (O3)
            sheltering the planet: the ozone shield
            deflecting into space
            the Sun's cell-slicing ultraviolet light.

Protected, single cells divide but don't leave home.
Individual cells organize themselves
                        as communities that carry on
                        (families, generations, histories)

Some stick together (to someday become plants)
                    safe inside shared, tough walls
                        learning to float or to live a lifetime in one place.
Some band together (to someday become animals),
                    share a flexible wall and rove around.
Others, fungi, assemble inside soft walls,
                        root in place
                        and spread for miles underground.

                    (The Earth's feeding wheel readies to turn:

                    Animals will eat and breathe
                            the bodies and breath of plants

fungi and bacteria will eat
plant and animal litter
to feed the plants.)

All the continents in the whole world
like bumper cars
driven by restless currents of the hot mantle
collide and meld
as one long tropical continent:
South America pushes into West Africa's great cove
East Africa, with India attached, rams Antarctica
Antarctica, fused to Australia, bonds with the west coast of
North America floating sideways near the South Pole

Rodinia   (Russian: "homeland")

Glaciers embrace the world, gleam back at the moon.

600 MILLION YEARS AGO

So slowly, slower than the eye can detect or the feet can feel,
the plates split again
(puzzle scattered, boats launched and sent back to sea)
torn apart by the molten mantle
churned by its own radioactive heat and the Earth's radiant core.

Antarctica tears away in a reluctant good-bye,
scarring North America with long, new, western rim,
stretching the rim as it pulls away
into a thin underwater wedge (San Bernardino to Las Vegas to Salt Lake City)
hundreds of miles wide and long
that sinks
toward the floor of a new ocean plate:
Ancestral Pacific
oozed through the long gash
between the rifting neighbors.

For millions of years
              seas advance and retreat across the Old West
      over the desert-dry continent
              all the way to Wisconsin
  leaving a rubble of rocks and dust
          washed by streams and rivers of rain
              or windblown
                  onto the continent's underwater ledge
                  or spilled onto the neighboring ocean plate
      to settle and collect on the emerging coast.

                  San Bernardino,
          the rocky left foot of North America,
                          trails in the ocean.

550 MILLION YEARS AGO
          Narrow North America bobbles sideways with the other continents
              all five strung along the equator
                  each a broad rough flat field
                      with wild seashores
                          and plenty of room for life.

Warm shallow seawaters flow
              onto North America from east and west
          retreat   flow inland over the flat land   retreat   flow

Sometimes the beach is in Utah.

Oxygen demands more and better breathers   gills
                                                hearts
                                                hemoglobin (oxygen-attracting iron
                                                    infused in primordial blood)

              Sea life abounds

Sudden, abundant, bigger!
In tropical seas,
Thronging trilobites scuttle—like seafloor cockroaches:

armored backs, antennae,
little tails, dozens of long legs

burrow in soft mud
near the seashore.

`

The beach is in Barstow and Needles.

New shapes and sizes abound
Worms, sponges, stalked clams, coral, and snails
Skeletons and shells, guts, fins, and jaws
The patterns of lives to come

An astounding flourish of life
We call it: The Cambrian Explosion!

Slow mysterious changes abound.
(Glaciers? Mystery)

Four times
sea levels fall and rise
warm sea water cools
and spreads over the continents.

A cold water pruning.

Most trilobite families and their warm-water neighbors   gone.

500 MILLION YEARS AGO
Warming   warming   warming

Rivers tumble out to sea
over algae-coated rocks in the coastal tide flats.

Flat and stable, warm, wet, and narrow
                              North America
                                        fused with Greenland and parts of Scotland

                    nods above and below the waters.

Rubble and dust settle in clean flat layers
                    (we will one day admire
                              after the Colorado River
                              cuts open the Grand Canyon).

Somewhere, in warm blue bays
by mutation (or mystery)
a nerve cord down the back of wormy sea animals
girdles in cartilage: vertebrates are born

Star-made calcium, phosphorus, and carbon
crystallize in the cartilage: bones are born.

450 MILLION YEARS AGO
In the temperate oceans encircling North America
                    the first little fish: *Astraspis*
                              six inches long, scaled
                              sucks its food from the shallow sea floor
                              along the coast of Colorado
                              where its body settles into silt after a lifetime
                              skimming the west coast, mating and feeding
                                        (to one day be dug up from its dirt bed,
                                        discovered by joyful scientists).

The gigantic continent Gondwanaland:
                    Southern Europe, Africa, South America, Antarctica, and Australia

          lush from millennia of tropical weather
                    floats across the South Pole and freezes.
                                        Ice Age worldwide.

Sea level drops in the world's oceans, baring shallow sea beds, ravaging marine families.

Most warm water life, withered and gone:

The Ordovician Extinction.

400 MILLION YEARS AGO

Eons of desolation,
                                        thaw,
                                                renewal.

Moss carpets the moist coastlines with delicate green fuzz.

Fungi and bacteria creep inland
        coast to coast across the brown continents.

In equatorial swamps and lowland floodplains
plants multiply shapes and sizes
        from green algae to branches to leaves
        to rooted and stemmed,
                encasing their trunks in tough fibers: wood.

The first trees rise thirty feet tall
        shading fern-thick undergrowth.

Fish swim in rivers and streams, scorpions
        and eight-inch-long millipede-like insects rustle
                                along the forest floor
                through dense plant litter.

From southern Idaho to Death Valley,
                a long beach laces the coast.

360 MILLION YEARS AGO
Slowly,
        slow and sure, over millions of years
                                to survive,
the first trees
        sex into male and female.

Male pollen wafts onto female plant-borne eggs

safe inside ovules that sheath
the seedling embryo with a tough cover
before shedding:
seeds.

Seeds, windborne, escape crowded riversides and wetlands
greening the dry interior.

Perhaps a meteor hit (mystery):

A white flow of glaciers
advances over Gondwanaland.

Serious global cooling. Sea levels drop.

Magnificent coral reefs and abundant reef life   gone
Seventy percent of marine animals   gone

Plant life on land
survives.

The Devonian Extinction.

After waves of desolation,
thaw,
rekindling,

renewal.

North America, fused to Europe, lolls at the equator.

One hundred-foot-tall fronded trees
and tall sweeping ferns grow

in vast swampy dense green forests
spreading inland along the waterways

leaving themselves behind, over millions of years,

from the middle of North America to the Black Sea
embedded in deep black layers
(we name:
coal).

Seven foot long millipedes, fungi, bacteria
digest the forest debris.

Insects buzz in the canopy, spiders weave their webs.

Dragonflies with two-foot wingspans,
waft iridescent among the greenery.

Sea urchins, sharks, starfish,
Salamanders, frogs, and toads.
Coral reefs and reef life abound.

A deep ocean plate,
butts hard
onto North America's long, wide,
low western wedge
and thrusts right over the top
pushing up the Antler Mountains
where we know Mono Lake, Nevada, southern Idaho
adding girth and grit to the West.

Rain and wind carry the mountains back to the sea,
eroding them to nearly nothing.
Seawater flows over the land.

4

Turritella, from Middle Miocene seabeds (16 to 12 million years ago):
Santa Monica Mountains.

Inland, on tropical North America,
                              by mutation, selection, (or mystery), over time and step by step
an amphibian mother—ancient unnamed water-wed relation—
discovers an able male and mates: internal fertilization
                                        the first amorous abandon stirs the gene pool
                                                    (marriage, divorce, telenovellas).
She lays in her nest a clutch of eggs, each one shell encased.
Inside, the embryos nestle in fluid-filled seawater sacks.

Amphibians transformed:
                              Reptiles are born.

A little reptile, lizard-like,
surveys the swamps in Kansas
                    where its relatives, the dinosaurs
                              will one day dawdle and feed.

280 MILLION YEARS AGO
Floating slowly east along the equator in warm dry weather
North America and Europe collide with Asia
                    welding a massive continent: Laurasia.

Near the South Pole floats gigantic Gondwanaland.

Like protons into atoms in the star furnace
Laurasia and Gondwanaland crash and fuse

          The bulge of West Africa rams southeastern North America
                    pushing up the Appalachians from Texas to Newfoundland
                              North America's tropical west coast
                                        faces north, looking out to sea.

(The puzzle put back together.)

One enormous continent:
                    Pangaea
                              (Greek: Gaea, Earth Mother of all,
                                        nourishing all
                                                  giving and taking
                                                        the lives of all)

floats in the universal ocean:

> Panthellasa

>> (Greek: Thalasa, Mother of Oceans and Fish
>> swimming in the great stream
>> encircling the whole world).

250 MILLION YEARS AGO

Far from moist ocean breezes
> Pangaea's immense center dries into a desert.

In the north (land we name eastern Russia) rising from the hot depths,
>> a massive plume of mantle heat
>>> dissolves the crust and bursts through fissures.
> Lava pouring for half a million years
>>> floods a million and a half square miles half a mile thick
> Sulfurous ash darkens the sky:
>>> the Siberian Traps.

Methane and carbon dioxide overwhelm the air.
Across Pangaea and in the newly acidic sea

>> oxygen breathers choke and die.

To the south,
> a six-mile-wide meteor explodes in the ocean
>> northwest of Australia
>>> blasts open 125 mile-wide Bedout crater:
>>>> tsunamis, ash, and smoke.

Temperatures plummet, then rise by eleven degrees.

> "The Great Dying" (Worst ever in the world)

We name it the Permian-Triassic Extinction
>> 70 percent of land life   gone
>> 95 percent of sea life   gone
Horned and fanged reptiles (the size of dogs and rhinoceros)
Corals, stalked clams, sea lilies, trilobites: gone   gone   all gone.

Photosynthesis drops.

Cockroaches survive.

For six million years,
            on near-barren Earth,
                        no more coal settles in its black beds.

On warm dry Pangaea
            water-laid amphibian spawn freeze, dry out, die.

            Reptiles resurge, lizard-like, growing larger,
                        and snakes and turtles
                                    all radiate madly across Pangaea.
            Their shell-encased eggs,
                        like seeds,
                                    survive the harsh weather.

Inland on the great continent
            fragile spores and primitive seeds,
                                    progeny of the first trees,
                        once wind-borne to incubate in moist swamps,
                        die as the swamps freeze or dry out.

The mantle wells up
                        hot and swirling
                        sliding a little thin edge of a newly arrived ocean plate
            under a slice of western North America's sea-covered ledge
                        (land we will one day call California)
            carrying it south, flowing toward Mexico.

                        The two plates slide past one another
                        two freight trains passing
                        for millions upon millions of days and nights.

The sea floor we know as Los Angeles
        arrives from San Francisco
        carried on the back of the ocean plate
What was here
        travels to Mexico.

Later, the mantle will drag this ocean floor
        part-way back from Mexico again
    back and forth,
        stretched and strewn into parts and pieces

           the coming Southern California coast.

240 MILLION YEARS AGO
          (Los Angeles is underwater.)

A giant ocean plate
        necklaced with volcanic islands
    plows into Western North America
        and piles right onto
        the old Antler Mountain rubble
        strewn on top of the continent's ancient wedge
The Sonomia Mountains rise
        and wear away to nearly nothing
    leaving themselves behind
        in deep mineral layers
          building the American West.

4   *Reptiles, Flowers, Mammals, Rivers*

Spreading east from a long crack
            in the ocean crust where magma flows forth
                                    like a ceaseless spring,
            a new ocean plate

pushes under western North America.

In accordance with their custom,
            it bends and dives under
                        descending, northeastward, beneath the continent
            to melt into the mantle.

Rubbed red-hot betwen the plates,
            magma pulses in fiery plumes
                                    through old seafloor sediments
                                    old mountain rubble

            cools to crystals   rises   cools to crystals   rises

                                    polished to giant pillows
                                    of black-speckled bright-white
            Mount Lowe granite
                        fifteen miles beneath the coming
                                    San Gabriel Mountains.

            More bold, massive granite globes

                                    laced with gold, copper, nickel, silver
                                    tourmaline, topaz, garnet

                        (treasure for the miners-to-come
                                    from the Earth's mineral essence
                                    from the forge of stars
                                    from the first proton
                                                from the birth of the universe)

line up like vertebrae (the Sierra Nevada to the tip of Baja)

gray, sparkling, deep-down spine of the coming mountain ranges.

Volcanoes burst the crust along the Old West Coast

fields of fireworks.

200 MILLION YEARS AGO
Magma swells through a long rift
                between West Africa and North America:

                Pangaea splits in two
                        opening the Atlantic Ocean,
                        pushing North America,
                                floating on its side near the equator, northwestward.

                The Gulf of Mexico opens as Africa carries east,
                        leaving behind rocks that are soon rendered
                        as a long limestone bar
                                        (we name: Florida).

                Over millions of years Pangaea will split again
                        and again and again
                        into continents (puzzle pieces scattered, the boats released,
                                once again sent back to sea).

North America:
                still attached to Eurasia across the north
                (Eurasia still attached to gigantic Gondwanaland)

a green and clement reptile paradise.

Dinosaurs, mostly small and swift,
                        running on two long back legs
        grow huge   huger   hugest
        grow wings, feathers, fins, horns, fangs, saber teeth, or bony crests
                stalk or scavenge, browse or kill

lay eggs in nests
tended in nurseries by mothers and fathers.

Round-ribbed, heavy-headed dinosaurs: rhino-like therapsids
        four-legged, short and stocky
        seeking safe territory for themselves
        migrating far south for millions of years
                into Gondwanaland's cool highland forests
                        (we call South Africa)

grow small   smaller smallest
        jaws and teeth for eating insects
        furred skin, warm-blooded
    tiny newborns, hatched from eggs, lick nourishing fluid oozed
    from sweat glands on their mother's chest:

Mammals are born
            nocturnal, shrew-sized (they would fit in a teaspoon)
                scurrying through the brush
                    climbing through the canopy.

165 MILLION YEARS AGO
The Jurassic   Dinosaur Era.

Right here:
        The beach is in Mohave.
        Los Angeles is underwater
                    on the continent's ledge

        It's a swampy bog life in warm shallow seas:
            clams, sea snails, sea urchins,
            cowrie shells, sand dollars, spiral nautilus
            star fish, scallops, mussels
            squid and oysters
            shrimp and crabs
                    a tasty bucket of life!

Teeming ammonites,
        coiled and chambered one inch to six foot shells
                    fishing with long tentacles

swim, feed, and die in Southern California seas.

Their calcium-rich shells pile and compact as limestone

                                          (mined to mix cement
to build sidewalks and shells
of buildings composed
as cities).

The bodies of large and small sea animals
      and dense green swamp plants
            die, rot, settle to the bottom in marine muds
covered and pressed, pressed and heated
layer upon layer of mud and dust thousands of feet deep
        heated and hardened
              into a layered black-gray stone (we name
                              Santa Monica Slate).

Fifty-foot-long high-speed Plesiosaurus, small head on a sea-serpent-neck,
        paddles along the shoreline

Thirty-foot-long sea lizards with little fins: Mosasaurs
        thick necks, large jaws, wide bodies
        flex and scull along the coast
        through Southern California seas.

                        (We find their bones near Fresno.
Relatives, the Fence Lizards,
sun themselves in our gardens.)

136 MILLION YEARS AGO
The Farallon, an ocean plate
      (where we recall the Pacific Ocean)
           thrusts northeastward
                farther, deeper under North America
          exploding more magma distilled to granite
                    that billows into the hard gray layers
                 of Santa Monica Slate.

Granite and slate: bedrock of what we will one day name
the Santa Monica Mountains.

(We see these dark slate ribs jut to the surface
on mountain tops.)

Somewhere in the world's dense forests, mammals stop laying eggs
and shelter fragile newborns in a belly-fold: marsupium
or inside the belly: womb
Mammal infants grow fat cheeks as
licking gives way to suckling
breasts.

Dreams are born in the minds of sleeping mammals.

100 MILLION YEARS AGO
For thirty million years, plants shed fertilizing pollen into the wind
or coat the legs of visiting insects,
come to drink the plant's sweet, nutritious nectar,
who carry the golden treasure to the next plant.

They carve a pact into the core of their lives:
plant + insect = life.

Then, one day, somewhere in the world's green expanse
in field or tropical forest
by mutation (or mystery): the first tiny petals
not green
now red, yellow, blue, pink
a glorious insect landing pad
and the first bees, butterflies, wasps
and, coming soon, the birds.

Mammals, chasing insects, discover fruits, nuts, seeds.

Dinosaurs chomp leaves, flowers, and their seed-filled fruits
and as they lumber along digesting,
poop seeds along the way.

A vegetarian duckbilled dinosaur
             (our local Hadrosaur)
                      thirty feet long
                      sixteen feet tall
                      long flat snout
                                mounted with a hollow bony crest for trumpeting to its mates
                                and hundreds and hundreds of teeth
            munches ferns, shrubs, pine branches, and fresh flowers
            migrates north on its big back legs,
                                          trailed by hungry Tyrannosaurus,
            to tend its young in nestling nurseries
                      and clambers south to die near San Diego
                      on a coastal plane
                                (that will one day rise as the Santa Ana Mountains).

The green continents are now florid.

                          North America: dazzling and buzzing!

80 MILLION YEARS AGO
In Southern California's
                      cool coastal waters
                      sharks sail by.

Hundred-pound ammonites with two-foot-wide shells
                rest along the coastline among snails and clams.

One-celled foraminifera, housed in miniscule shells
                like tiny secrets, gambol by the coast.

Suddenly speeding northeastward faster than it sinks
             flattening the angle of its crawl beneath North America
                                the Farallon Plate
             spurts massive rounds of magma
                      deep into the old rocks fifteen miles underground
                                where later will rise
                                Mt. Waterman, Mt. Wilson, Mt. Josephine
             distilling Mt. Josephine granite

                (fine grained, glowing, gray-pink face of the coming San Gabriel Mountains).

Volcanoes fire off all the way to the new-rising Rockies.

Far away beneath the ocean near what we call Australia
      magma gushes from a long, ancient crack in the crust:
                            the East Pacific Rise.

The bubbling flow keeps coming, fills in,
        Piles high into ridges on both sides of the gash,
        slides down both ridges (gravity rules!),
hardens in cold ocean waters,

        filling and sliding   filling and sliding
growing continents on each side of the gash (two inches a year).

One side: The gigantic Farallon Plate
                 pushing beneath North America
                    leaves scrapings of itself
                       on the continent's edge
                          building Southern California.

Flowing from the other side, its deep ocean twin: The Pacific Plate,
      smaller, but fast growing north
                    faster, fatter.

65 MILLION YEARS AGO
Pangaea splinters as new oceans open wide.

The continents (soon to be shaped as we know them) push on
                    covered and uncovered as they wander
                      by warm, shallow seas.

        Propelled by the widening Atlantic
        North America, like a great ship, plows northwest from the tropics
                  (where Puerto Rico now lies)
        arcs north (as far north as South Dakota) and turns southwest.

5

"Fearsome Bear" (*Phoberogale shareri*), the first species of bear to arrive in North America,
is the predecessor of modern bears, dogs, and sea lions. Only as tall as a medium-sized
dog, it was adapted for running in open country. This skull is about 20 million years old:
northern Santa Ana Mountains. Specimen courtesy of Vertebrate Paleontology Collection,
Natural History Museum of Los Angeles County. Special thanks to Xiaoming Wang, curator,
Department of Vertebrate Paleontology, Natural History Museum of Los Angeles.
The specimen belongs to the Orange County Paleontologic Collection (OCPC).

The west coast at the prow of the continent.

(Los Angeles underwater.)

Sea level drops, sea currents slow and shift wildly.
The weather grows hot and wet.
Plankton and coral reefs in the coastal bays near Mojave die.

India rips away from Africa over a hot spot
Boiling magma bolts to the surface

spreading lava a mile-thick across 800,000 square miles:
the Deccan Plateau.

Red-orange fiery fountains, spewing sparks

shoot ash into the stratosphere.

Carbon dioxide, sulfurous rain, ash, and dust clot the air worldwide.

Lava, smoke, steam blow for a million years (and the spot still simmers).

Blared and booming,
an astral mountain nine miles wide

rockets—one hundred thousand miles per hour—into the Gulf of Mexico

blasting a crater sixty-two miles wide and eighteen miles deep
(Chicxulub: The Devil's Tail).

Black out, earthquake magnitude eleven, tsunami, acid rain,
shocked quartz and minerals melted to glass beads
scatter over Southern California's bays and beaches
all the way across the continent and the Caribbean.
Firestorms rage through the Southwest.

Vaporized, the meteor rains its rare element, iridium, worldwide.

Seventy-five percent of everything dies.

Southern California's lush woodlands and flowering plains   gone

Duck-billed Hadrosaurs with their mouths full of pine needles,
                    and sea-going Plesiosaurs and Mosasaurs   gone

Worldwide, the grand reptile giants: gone   gone   completely gone.

Sea-going, coiled ammonites: completely gone.

                    Life shaped in smaller bodies survives:

Snakes, lizards, turtles, crocodiles, insects, and some dinosaurs-become-birds.

Nocturnal, cat-sized mammals peek out from undercover
                              and spread into the dino-liberated world.

The breeze blows warm in the worldwide greenhouse.

Ferns grow back first.

Then seeds sprout; flowers glow through the green.

Leaf-shedding tropical forests flourish and migrate
                    south to Southern California's wet-weathered, swampy coast.

Right here: Evidence of the great disaster
                         rain-washed away off the rising mountains
                         or melted with the Farallon back to magma under North America.

50 MILLION YEARS AGO
The world is greenhouse warm.

Alligators bask beneath Canadian palms; tropical Britain is hot and green.

Waves curl and warm seawaters crest across the Mojave
                                   and flood the Baja borderlands
In the shallows: snails, clams, crabs, sea urchins.

Sharks sail by (their teeth lie buried in Simi Valley).

Gobbled up, nearly gone
the Farallon slows and takes a steep plunge

                                deeper under North America

Magma's upwelling hot bald heads push through the cracks and stretch the crust
        and the West expands
          from the new Rockies to the old west coast.

Volcanoes flare! ash clouds! lava!
        gaping calderas   bubbling mudpots   stinking fumerols

As the Farallon slows
        a long, wide coastal plain (where we envision Baja—
        land we will name Southern California)
                rises out of the water.

Rivers braid across this new territory
          carrying river-borne sand and cobbles to fattening deltas.

Pine trees flourish along a luxurious, thick-forested coastline
Broad-backed aquatic rhinoceroses and very long crocodiles
                wallow in warm wetland shallows
Monkeys, lemurs, and mouse-sized opossums clamber in the magnolias,
        palms, figs,
           guava, beech, maple,
             walnut, redwood, oak, and sycamore
Camels (the size of collie dogs) and tapirs browse the underbrush.

Saber-toothed cats hunt the newly hoofed
        pig-, cow-, horse-, cattle-, deer-like mammals
        all wandering to Eurasia and back again
        across the warm, redwood-forested Arctic.

Hyena-like carnivores pursue pronghorn-like antelope
      across wet-weather fields

where broad muddy rivers meander through wetlands into a deep bay
we will name the Santa Ana Mountains.

(Some of this land, later shifted and transported,
we will use to dump our trash:
the Simi Valley landfill.)

In the Mojave, turtles sun on the shores of lakes and streams.

Local whales ply the coast,
toothed, short-limbed swimmers
already in the water for ten million years.

36 MILLION YEARS AGO

Flare!   Blam!
Meteors careen into
Chesapeake Bay, Virginia (sixty-mile-wide pit)
Anabar Plateau, Russia (sixty-two-mile-wide pit)
Ash and dust darken the skies.
The weather cools.

Gondwanaland already splintered:
India, Australia, Africa,
South America unhitches Antarctica
and they all float north,
leaving Antarctica
stranded and cooling
at the South Pole

opening a path (Drake's Passage) for cold currents
to circle round and round and round the polar continent.

Temperate Antarctica's moist mammal-lively forests—oaks and ferns—
dying.

Glaciers spread across Antarctica
sea waters freeze and separate:
fresh water ice rises to the surface
and the heavy, salt-laden sea water sinks

and seeps north in deep, frigid currents
cooling all the waters they contact

Sea level falls hundreds of feet.

Cold water cools the air.

Around the world the weather chills.
Tropical warm and wet shifts to seasonal cool and dry.

Mammal extinctions:

La Grand Coupure/The Great Cut

Mojave to Baja: thick shoreline forests:
gone.

Woodlands open where the forests once stood.

Sharp-clawed, strong jawed giant predators:
completely gone
except hyena-like pack hunters and the small carnivores.

Southern California's grand mammal panoply,
the forest leaf browsers large and small:
gone
or evolved to grazers with high crowned teeth.

Horses peer above the greenery, gallop to safety on longer legs.

Ravens,
immigrant flocks flown to Southern California from Eurasia
survive the cut.

28 MILLION YEARS AGO

Right here
the magma-welling East Pacific Rise,
birthplace of the vanished Farallon,
stalls, rolled over by
the west coast of North America (on its slow turn southwest).

The Farallon,
                  gravity-drawn down under North America for millions of years,
completely melted and consumed,
                    except for two huge sinking slabs:
                         The Juan de Fuca, still vanishing
                              beneath the Northwest
                              (Eureka, Portland, Seattle)
                         The Rivera, still rumbling under
                              Southern Mexico, Central America

and a few, small unsinkable tailings

All the rest vanished into the mantle
                    to one day rise again as magma through volcanoes
                    and cracks between the plates.

The Farallon's bouncy tail end,
                    the final flounce of its magnificent skirt,
            formed from the last of its magma
            freshly shed, thin, and light,
         buoys the land above it.

               Near places we name San Diego and the Orocopia Mountains:
               the San Gabriel and Peninsular Mountains begin to rise.

                    (Mounts Pinos, San Antonio/"Old Baldy," San Jacinto:
                      mountains where we will one day stand
                             overlooking—ahh!—a sea of lights.)

Uplifted and flushed by rainwater, once deeply rooted rocks,
                    ancient gneiss, anorthosite, granite,
                 roll downhill in rivers and streams
                        cobbles and boulders collect in deep foothill fans
                        and sandy river deltas

Wind and rain wash the new land
                turned rust red as its mineral iron

meets the oxygenated air
down to the new coast.

Camels and horses, rhino and hippopotamus-like browsers nibble,
gophers tunnel, small and large dogs snooze,
rabbits, squirrels, and mice scamper through the shrubbery.

With the Farallon subducted and out of its way,
the Pacific Ocean Plate
slowly growing
driving steadily north
then shifting northwest over a hotspot
(the Hawaiian Islands),
deep underwater
touches North America right here
(Los Angeles, California)

abrading its way
along the western rim of California
northwest
to the Aleutian Islands
where it bends and dives down into a long trench
melting under Asia and into the mantle
swirled away
to someday rise again as magma.

And so the raw edge between the two plates—the San Andreas Fault—settles in

marking the border
where the two plates (like lovers)
shape and reshape one another.

25 MILLION YEARS AGO

Where we envision San Diego and Northern Baja: a verdant expanse of North America
rising mountain ridges and a wide coastal slope,
river-wet grasslands, mud-flats, oyster beds
ebbed and flooded by Pacific Ocean tides.

6

Deformed strata caused by motion
on the nearby San Andreas fault: Palmdale.

A dying whale,
  long snout and fat ribs
  teeth and baleen strainers
sinks into sea sediments
    (we discover near Lake Casitas).

Here lies the magnificent reach of land,
    that will one day twirl ninety degrees as it's carried northwest
  to stretch and sink, crumple and rise
    into the plains, mountains, and valleys we will name:

    Point Conception, Cuyama Valley, Mount Pinos, Mount Frazier,
    Santa Ynez Mountains and Valley, Santa Barbara,
    Los Angeles Basin, San Fernando and San Gabriel Valleys,
    Santa Monica, Santa Susana,
    Verdugo and San Gabriel Mountains,
    Channel Islands.

It is very warm.

Inland springs and streams from mountains deep in North America
    flow (over land we will someday name
      Southwest Arizona and the Mojave Desert)
  spill (through what we will someday name
      the Orocopia Mountains and Lockwood Valley—
      land connected, but soon splintered and transported)
collect
  as the powerful
      North River.

Its driving current clefts the rising mountains

      (Sierra Pelona   San Gabriel)

    cuts, widens, deepens a river valley
bends north,

spills into a verdant delta
                (we will name the Cuyama Valley)
                      and empties into the Pacific.

Sand sifts down to riverbed,
        packed layer after layer, pressed into sandstone
        that will one day tilt, exposing a bristle of boulders
        (Vasquez Rocks).

But a rising new mountain range (we call it Frazier-San Gabriel)
        splits the North River
          and some of its waters
          flow down the other side of the rising highland:

              the South River

     into a deep coastal bay.

The new South River
      spills through San Gorgonio Pass,
            (casinos, plaster dinosaurs, Interstate 10)
     courses through uplifting mountains, gathers into lakes,
        filters through a sprawling wetland delta and washes into
          thriving seaside tide flats in northern Baja.
          (We will find its layers
              in the Santa Monica and Santa Ana Mountains.)

7
Vazquez Rocks: Agua Dulce.

5   *Southern California Coming: Mountains in Motion*

Right here, the relentless Pacific Plate,

                  drags out from under North America

                  the tail end of the old Farallon:

      The Monterey Microplate

                        and welds it to its side.

And so the Monterey Microplate, one with the Pacific, begins its journey northwest.

As the Pacific Ocean Plate—

        plowing along its pathway,

                  the San Andreas Fault—

    drags away its cargo: the captured microplate,

    the fabric of western North America stretches behind it

                  all the way to the Rockies.

Thin and stressed, the land sinks and ripples

          into broad valleys and low mountain ridges

          we name the Basin and Ranges.

Nevada doubles in size.

Where we recall the Antelope Valley of the Mojave Desert,

            westernmost reach of the Basin and Ranges,

       the east sliding Garlock Fault

     and the northwestward San Andreas converge

    (an arrowhead sharpened to a point).

        The point will pierce the Sierra Nevada

            and rend its granite spine.

Vigorously dragged along the San Andreas,

    the broad tail end of the Sierra Nevada

           (Tehachapi Mountains)

SOUTHERN CALIFORNIA COMING: MOUNTAINS IN MOTION

curls around the southern curve of a long deep bay
                              (the San Joaquin Valley).
              As it warps and smears northwest,
                    its ancient granites lie like trail markers along the San Andreas.
                              (We see their gleam in the Coast Range.)

As the Pacific Plate cracks off and carries away more western rim
        the San Andreas Fault breaks northwest all the way
        to Point Arena's triple junction
                    where Pacific, North America, Juan de Fuca Plates
                                        (still) tussle.

Sea lions, relatives of the bears, bask on the beach
                              near Bakersfield.

Immigrant sagebrush and the dry weather plants
        traveling from Wyoming
        finally reach Nevada and put down roots.

The coastline subsides and sea level rises.
                        Along the Baja borderlands,
            the seashore moves inland as the mountains wear down.

Ocean floods the river deltas.

Waves curl against the foothills of rising Mount Pinos.

                    Three times the sea rises and recedes.

Clams and small spiral Turritella nestle in the silty seafloor.

                    (Along Old Topanga Highway, their mud-crusted shells
                    poke through the old sea bottom
                    now lifted into ridge tops in the Santa Monica Mountains.

What was below is above,
given over to sun, wind
and the rain that washes it all downstream
given over to the bulldozer's blade,
the fossil seeker's eager trowel.)

The North and South Rivers unceasingly wash down their canyons
piling the shore,
filling their canyons with dirt, stones, and sand.

16 MILLION YEARS AGO
Squirming, creeping
deep beneath the Southern California coast
the Pacific Ocean Plate,
merged with the Monterey Microplate,

tears and heaves until finally

the Monterey Microplate

crumbles into great blocks

jostling and twirling as they travel northwest.

One huge hunk (we name the Western Transverse Ranges Block) torn off,
shudders and lets go,

mountains, hills, islands, valleys, rivers and streams
(Point Conception, the northern Channel Islands,
Santa Barbara, Ventura, Santa Monica Mountains, Simi Valley)
carried away in one piece by the Pacific Ocean Plate.

First the great Block hauls northwest
sliding along the fathomless channel,
the San Andreas Fault,
stressing and stretching the land behind it.

But its bow sticks tight
                      against the Frazier-San Gabriel Mountains Block—
                              another huge chunk dragging up the San Andreas—
near the granite core of Mount Gleason
       and won't let go.

Rocky moorings shredded, asunder,
                the wayward block, relentlessly pulled,
                      pivots at that point

        cracked off, broken away
        its stern (Point Conception) swings clock-wise away from the Baja coast,
                its tail-end swirled around
                      by the streaming Pacific Plate.

            (And so the stern of the Block becomes its bow.
                        Point Conception leads the way.)

The Block cracks off right through the South River canyon
and the canyon thins and slowly fans open
                  ever-widening, bursting volcanoes
                  as the great Block tears away.

Submarine volcanoes rip and roar
piling up lava (where we will one day walk
                in the Santa Monica Mountains)

In the widening, sinking, ever-stretching, sea-flooded basin
           lava layers into mountains we will name
           Santa Catalina, San Clemente Islands.

Stretched thin, the coastal crust
                  can't hold down the hot minerals beneath it.
The Monterey Microplate, remnant of the old Farallon,
                    long ago dragged by the Pacific Plate
                  out from under North America
                  where its seafloor sediments were cooked
                  to a glossy green glass stone: Catalina Schist,

                        pops toward the surface
                                lifts into islands and highlands

                        to be weather-fractured and washed
                                downhill by rivers and streams.

(Rock hounds gather the green-glassy stones
                heaped in the Santa Monica Mountains,
                on the Catalina Island, San Onofre seashores.)

Volcanoes blast across the coming Southern California landscape.
Lava from the new volcanoes flows over the schist.

(The basin we will call Los Angeles: a new coastal seabed bursting volcanic islands.)

Conejo Mountain builds high and mighty:
                                        a towering volcano five thousand feet tall
Cypress and Douglas Fir forests thrive on its magnificent flanks.

(We see its basalt heart, a round hill rising by Highway 101, near Oxnard.)

At the North Pole the weather is cool: ice caps, glaciers
                glaciers world-wide
                glaciers in the Sierra Nevada
The weather at the equator cools.

Mantle currents carry South America into isolation.
Its contact with North America stops.

Once wet Southern California summers
                grow warm and dry
                        rainy winters turn cooler

Tropical forests thin
the magnolias and the tulip trees   gone

Lush-forest-loving primates—monkeys and lemurs—and the marsupials:
completely gone.

Dry summer-weather grasslands, seeding their way west, Wyoming to Nevada,
finally gain the coast
slowly sheath coastal hills

Oaks, laurel, madrone, avocado dot the rising hillsides
Sycamores, alders, cottonwoods retreat to stream sides

Greening the highlands: pine, fir, sequoia

Horses, camels, the new rhinos—with teeth good for grazing rough fodder—flourish
Rats, mice, lizards, and snakes carry on in the fields among the spare trees

Snakes brandish their brand new rattles.

Nine-foot-tall, four-tusked mastodons (the Gomphotheres)
And two-tusked mastodons
wander over from Asia and return

back and forth   back and forth   back and forth

from Asia, Europe, Africa,
the grazers find the Southern California shoreline.

In the open terrain, good grazers grow larger, taller and longer-legged:

Seven kinds of horses
camels short and tall
the first true pronghorn antelope
race over open country
hop across the savannah.

Three kinds of saber-toothed cats
hyenas and big dogs and
Amphicyan: tiger-like with the face
of a dog and the body of a bear
hunt deer-like, pig-like, and sheep-like grazers.

Owls, eagles, and hawks
hunt squirrels, rabbits, and hedgehogs.

Gulls, egrets, cormorants, albatross,
pink flamingoes with glossy black beaks
flock in abounding coastal waters
Osteodontornis: the bony-toothed bird
   eighteen-foot wingspan,
   razor zig-zagged sixteen-inch beak
   snags fish and squid.

Ravens and crows feast on what they find.

Whales—three kinds
  sea lions with long toes and claws
  seals
  dolphins
  and the giant walruses
  sea-loving crocodiles and the first sea otters
  sea cows the size of elephants:
    head like a horse, body like a walrus,
    wades on shore like a hippopotamus with short fat legs
    scooping mollusks and seaweed
    with their four tusks.

All swimming, feeding, dying
  their bones settling
  into land we will one day name
      Bonita Canyon near MacArthur Boulevard
      the Palos Verdes Peninsula
      suburban Calabasas
      the lawns of Leisure World.

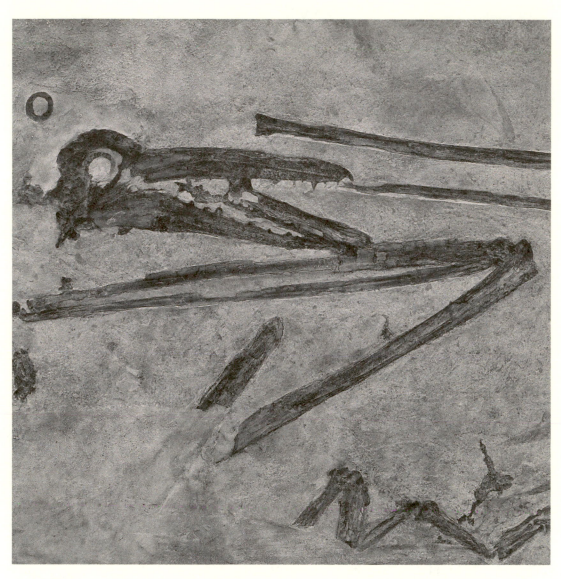

8

Bony-toothed bird (*Osteodontornis orri*). In 1957, preeminent avian paleontologist Hildegarde Howard announced the discovery of a complete skeleton with feather impressions on opposing slabs of shale. It had an 18- to 20-foot wingspan and a bony beak lined with tooth-like projections. Dated to the middle Miocene (about 16 to 12 million years ago): Santa Barbara County. A cast of the Santa Barbara Museum holotype, this specimen is courtesy of Vertebrate Paleontology Collection, Natural History Museum of Los Angeles County.

Camels and antelope browse under oaks and juniper
mastodons and mice sun themselves beneath the palm trees.

Near Bakersfield, sharks glide by.

13 MILLION YEARS AGO
Earthly giants sail northwest

    the broad back of the Pacific Plate
        merged with the Monterey Microplate,

    and the loosed smaller blocks.

Southern California's rising mountains
        wend through coastal waters
        catching the rain and sea winds
          like slow billowing
            dark blue sails.

Battered and stretched tight to breaking,
    the weakened San Gabriel Block cracks and a fault opens
        between the Frazier and San Gabriel Mountains
        rifting the two ranges that once rose side by side.

Liberated, the new Frazier Mountain Block
        creeps northwest along the new fault,
          leaving behind the San Gabriel Mountains
          (now risen three thousand feet beside the Orocopia Mountains)
        and slides right across and dams the North River.

A lake collects (Mint Canyon).

Hauled northwest right on past Mint Canyon, the Frazier Mountain Block
      releases the lake and the sea flows in.

          The beach is in Castaic.

As the Western Transverse Ranges Block rumbles and twirls northwest,
      the canyon once cut by the old South River
          stretches ever thinner as the Block continues its clock-wise turn,

    fanned wider, stretched thinner
          it sinks into a deep coastal bay:

          the Los Angeles Basin
               sea-filled
                  dazzling blue.

As the flimsy canyon floor sinks
          it ripples into underwater basins
     where round pin-tip-sized
         snowflake sea animals, diatoms,
               nestle.

Shrimp eat the diatoms.
Whales eat the shrimp.

A thirty-two-foot-long baleen whale dies, sinks
belly up and settles at the bottom of the bay.

      (Lincoln Heights
          a man in an orchard digging a ditch
          hits rock that stops his shovel: whale bones

      Mt. Washington
          a man walking a dog stumbles;
          thick in the sandstone: whale bones.)

Diatom skeletons pile like snowdrifts
      (diatomaceous earth)

Their soft innards settle to the bottom of the bay,
      decay in dense layers
covered by thousands of feet of dirt and dust
covered and pressured to methane
            and a black carbon goo:

gas

tar

oil

    right here.

Streams of rain pour off the rising Southern California mountain ranges
     rolling sand, dirt, rocks into the bay
          slowly pushing the ocean back.

5.8 MILLION YEARS AGO

Africa, tugged north for millions of years by the mantle current,
     pins Morocco to Spain
     sealing the Mediterranean Sea.
Cut off from the Atlantic
     the Mediterranean evaporates into rain
       greens to grassland, fills again, dries to salt, fills, dries to salt
       and dies in a salt-laden waste

Massive rains dilute the world's saline seas
     the rain-fresh water, flowing north, easily freezes

Broadening fields of white ice
     reflect sunlight back into space

Earth's temperature spirals down, cooler and cooler

Polar ice caps grow deep and spread seaward

The world's warm weather madly swings: cold, colder, warmer, colder
                                 for four hundred thousand years
The first salvo of a slow chill.

                          (Later, near Gibraltar, when the world warms up,
                          seawater breaks a channel that rips into a torrent:
                          Gibraltar Falls—one thousand times Niagara Falls,
                          floods and refills the Mediterranean Sea.)

Subtropical Southern California cooling down.

5 MILLION YEARS AGO
The six continents
                  catch rays, linger in their (now familiar) positions.

Plowing northwest while they're squeezed up
                         between the San Gabriel and San Andreas faults,
      the San Gabriel Mountains
leave behind their companions, the Orocopia Mountains
                            (still standing beside the Salton Sea).

Streams and springs flowing from mountains deep in the continent
                        no longer find the North River canyon,
                        its cleft shifted away
                                northwest with the San Gabriel Mountains.

      But local mountain streams and springs find
      its ancient wide-open river path

      braid across the land
                     (that will soon rise as the Santa Susana Mountains)
      and empty through wetlands into a coastal bay
                     (the coming San Fernando Valley).

                  (Waters have flowed wild
                      through this venerable river canyon,

now home to the Santa Clara,
for twenty million years.)

The beach is in Newhall.

Bears, long-limbed, land-running, twice as tall as polar bears
wander over from Asia
snuffle blackberries along the North River.

The great craft of broken-away continent,
the Western Transverse Ranges Block,
spun ninety degrees
slows its twirl (still twirling)
as Point Conception and all the rest
docks (where we recall Santa Barbara)
widening the Southern California coastline by miles.

In its wake a wide teeming bay (the Los Angeles Basin)
salves the rift where it once tore away.

9

Whale effigy. This tiny steatite whale effigy
was recovered in 1958. Effigies of whales,
pelicans, cormorants, fish, sea otters, seals,
and dophins as well as phallic wands are found
mostly on the Channel Islands or along the
coast. Discovered in burials or ceremonial
caches, they date from the earliest period
of occupation which now extends to 13,000
years ago: Channel Islands. Courtesy of the
Southwest Museum of the American Indian,
Autry National Center of the American West,
Los Angeles; 1521.G234A.

Twirled and sliding, bumped and grinding
                              ever northwest
The Frazier Mountains shift
                              past the west-bent end of the southern Sierra
The San Gabriel Mountains

                              squeezed higher and tilted up
                              between the San Andreas and San Gabriel Faults
                              line up behind the Frazier Mountains.

Relentless, the Pacific Plate
            still coursing under North America's southwestern rim
            steals with one long slice, the Baja Block:
                  Peninsular Mountains, San Diego, Baja all the way to its tip:

                              The Baja Transfer

The San Andreas breaks from Palmdale to Mexico
                        (through the gap we name Cajon Pass)
stranding in North America
                  the San Bernardino and Orocopia Mountains
stretching a canyon that slowly
                  deepens (Coachella Valley, Palm Springs, the Salton Sea).

Deep below, the old East Pacific Rise, a scar re-severed,
                              vents magma once again
                              piling up new seafloor that steadily widens
                              the new Sea of Cortez
                              severing Baja from mainland Mexico

Earthquakes! Volcanoes!

Baja, a long, slim barge
                  with its freight of mountains, valleys, rivers, and plains
                  dragged by the Pacific Plate
                        heads out northwest
                              along the San Andreas.

The collection of chunks and hunks we call Southern California,
                    its lot cast with the Pacific Plate,
        all jostle up the San Andreas's seven hundred and forty miles,
        usually crawling two inches a year
                        sometimes lunging twenty feet or more

                (In ten million years Los Angeles will sail by San Francisco
                still stranded on North America's shore.)

        toward a trench bordering the Aleutian Islands
        where the Pacific Plate dives under
                and melts into the mantle
                            to one day rise again as magma
                    burst through volcanoes and cracks between the plates.

The ground is so stressed,
            it frays into strands of smaller faults:
            Santa Monica-Malibu, Newport-Inglewood, Verdugo, Whittier,
            and many more.

Fault-vented heat boils underground streams to the surface:
hot springs percolate across Southern California.

            (Indigenous people, for millennia,
            heal and calm in the warm mineral waters,
                waters we cap and send to sewers
                    or pipe to spas
                    near Ojai, West Hollywood, Palm Springs;
                        in Encino, warm water from capped springs
                            burbles into the Los Angeles River.)

3.5 MILLION YEARS AGO

Volcanoes blast and rain follows
            on the savannah (Laetoli, East Africa)

Three primates, each upright on two legs, make tracks
            across a wet ash field, sinking in

middle-size feet step carefully
                    into prints of larger feet
        hurrying along, at arms length, keeping up: small feet.

Drying ash cements the prints.

3 MILLION YEARS AGO
India, thrust into Eurasia for millions of years,
                    shoves harder, continent into continent:
                                        towering overrides, thrusts, warps, and crumblings
The Himalayas billow toward five-miles-high
            blocking, shifting monsoons and the tropical jet stream.

The Tibetan plateau freezes to an ice desert
                                        shining sunlight back into space.
Ice sheets advance as the North Atlantic shivers.

            The world cools   heats   cools.

Along the Southern California coast
                    warm summer rains stop falling.

Plants seeking survival
                    cling to scattered local niches
In the highlands,
            oak, avocado, walnut disperse among the grasses
A sagebrush chaparral of dry weather plants
                                invades the coastal lowlands

Moist, subtropical, green leafy bushes wither,
                    opening grassy fields of coarse fodder

        The last subtropical-leaf-browsing horses, camels,
                    and all the other browsers: completely gone.

        Pronghorns and the grazing horses flourish

        Heads-up leaf feeders gone; heads-down grass feeders thrive.

Cooler winds blow across grassy fields.

South America, drifting west,
     nears North America's slim southern tail end

Into the narrow gap between the continents
  volcanoes blast and build to mountains lifting above the water:
    The Isthmus of Panama
        plugs the path between Pacific
        and tropical Atlantic currents.

    Warm waters and their rain-rich clouds
    now must curl through the Caribbean, circle Florida
    and flow into the Gulf Stream
    warming the North Atlantic
    where seawater evaporates and returns as snow.

  Blazing out of the blue
    the Eltanin Meteor, over half a mile wide,
      smashes into the South Pacific.
Exploded seafloor and ancient fossils
  fall back in heat-melted jumbles; debris-laden clouds
  burden the cooling cycle.

    Snow piles high and higher in the far north.
    Arctic ice caps thicken to thousands of feet.

Across the new Isthmus of Panama, wandering north
  ramble South American:
    porcupines, opossums, sloths, armadillo-like glimtadons (larger than a desk)
    monkeys, anteaters,
    teratorns (twelve-foot wingspan) wing their way

      to Southern California's grasslands

Across the Isthmus of Panama traveling south
        trek North American:
                elephants, horses, camels, skunks,
                bears, rabbits, deer, cats and dogs

        back and forth   back and forth   back and forth

        growing taller, longer, bigger, wider as they travel.

The granite spine of the Sierra Nevada
        hard pushed from underneath

                (ancient rocks to the top:
                 gray rain-washed old bones exposed)

        tilts sharply, sinks west toward the San Joaquin Sea,
        flaunting its glittery underpinnings:
                granite lifted as an east-facing wall (sheerest, highest in the world)

        The southern mountains soar tallest (Mt. Whitney rises, a mountain waking)

        Clouds from the coast halt against the ascending Sierra
        On the east side, mountain runoff
                        flowing through dry weather grasslands
                        streams into Owens Lake.

                        (We remember Mulholland,
                         lawnmowers, gutters full of runoff,
                         Hockney pools, birds of paradise.)

The Western Transverse Mountain Ranges—Point Conception to the Cajon Pass—
                        pivoted and pulled northwest along the San Andreas
        stall in a pocket where the great fault,
                blocked

               by the granite mass of the San Bernardinos

      bowed

              by the granite spine of the southern Sierra,

    curves west ("The Big Bend")

And so the Western Transverse Mountain Ranges

                     all line up with the San Bernardinos

              that beacon across the fault from North America.

Momentarily (the long moment we call the present)

        one mountain range

                 spans Southern California east and west:

        the Western and Eastern Transverse Ranges.

Mt. San Gorgonio, caught between the tight left turn of the

        the San Andreas as it bends past the San Bernardino Mountains

          rises higher, highest.

A wide blue bay laps against the Frazier and San Gabriel Mountains

      north to Ventura

      south to the Santa Ana Mountains.

Plowing north, the long, narrow mountainous barge,

                Baja Peninsula,

rams straight into the east-west wall of the slowed Western Transverse Mountain Ranges

               as they drag along the San Andreas.

Jammed by Baja into the Big Bend, the ground (we call Los Angeles)

        cracks into slabs and

        grit blocks, bashed and squeezed,

        tilt and sink—bellies uplifted like old ships—

        or crumple into new mountain ridges, new valleys

        all running east and west.

Fractured, the ground frays into more faults:

Northridge, Mission, San Fernando, Santa Susana, Santa Ynez

At the Santa Monica-Malibu Fault
            the Santa Monica Mountains, slowly squeezed,
            fold and tilt out of the water:
                        the bottom of the bay is the top of the mountain.

Thrust up or folded along the faults:
            Verdugo Mountains, Puente, and Hollywood Hills
            slowly rise out of the water.

Where we recall Moorpark, Thousand Oaks, and the Simi and San Fernando Valleys,
            a coastal bay
                        ripples around the rising mountains.

As the Pacific Plate thrusts Baja into the Western Transverse Mountain Ranges
            the ground shifts, splits, buckles, folds
                        one chunk thrusts over another
                                                valleys sink
                                                mountains rise
            as the ground quakes (still quaking)

            deep booming from the two plates' grinding slide,
                        quartz rocks squeezed between the slabs
                        flash like ball lightning.

San Gabriel Mountains: one of the fastest rising mountain ranges on Earth.
San Fernando Valley,
                        hard pressed between rising mountain ranges
                                    (will one day narrow to a canyon).

Rain rolls down mountains in rivers and streams
            filling the great Southern California bay with rocks washed off
                        once deep rooted, now up-tilted mountain tops.

10

Fossil scallop shells. Dating from the middle Miocene (16 to 12 million years ago),
these large mollusks lived in shallow sea waters: Topanga Canyon.

6 *Southern California Ice Age:*
Bountiful Homeland

Waves curl over the beach at Nordoff Street
            (in the soon-to-be San Fernando Valley).

The Santa Clara River still flows through the ancient North River canyon
                        spun with its mountains ninety degrees
                        transported northwest one hundred and ninety miles
                                    (still traveling)
                                flooding a wide green delta
                    over the coming Santa Susana Mountains
                    and San Fernando Valley.

Sand and river-rounded stones
                piled, covered, pressed
                for a million years
harden as sandstone bars and bulges
                        and river-rock hodgepodge
                that will one day soon
            tilt into low mountain ridges.

Horses and deer, tapirs and mastodons browse and graze by the river's edge.

Palos Verdes: an island
                in a coastal bay lapping at the base
                of the rising San Gabriel Mountains.

Catalina, San Nicolas, Santa Barbara, San Clemente Islands
                tramp along their faults
                        northwest with the mountain ranges.

Seaside plains sweep like wings from the mountain peaks (we name)
                San Miguel, Santa Rosa, Santa Cruz, Anacapa Islands
            sailing by inches
                    beside the coastline (we name Santa Barbara).

Albatross soar over the islands.
Beaked whales and great white shark wend their way.

Cooler.

Antarctic currents chill the floor of the world's oceans.
Arctic ice sheets thicken.

The Earth, on its yearly elliptical journey,
        sails close by the sun during northern hemisphere winter
                        (wet, snowfall)
        far away during northern hemisphere summer
                        (snow sticks to the ground)

And one day, wobbling as it does on its axis,
        straightens up a little: less sunlight strikes the snowy north

Temperatures drop

        old glaciers fatten

        glistening ice and snow fields gleam sunlight back into space.

                The air cools.

New winter snows, still frozen through cooler summers,
        pack mile-high into glaciers

                their dense cold burden creeps downhill,
                        bulldozing with their ice blades
                        a till of shattered rock
                and their massive bodies sink deep,
                        grind rocks to powder,
                        pluck and carry boulders hundreds of miles,
                        sharpen mountain peaks
                        deepen, smooth, and widen valleys

seawater sucked into ice:

                                  sea level falls four hundred feet

Ice Age.

Glaciers coat North America
          in the west all the way to Oregon
          New York all the way over Manhattan
          (Central Park under half a mile of ice)
and, melting, shed torrential floods
scouring river courses, lake basins

Glaciers and the frozen land link continents:
Eurasia (across the Bering Strait) to North America to Greenland.

Temperatures pulse in cycles:

warm melt freeze   warm melt freeze   warm melt freeze

every one hundred thousand years (still pulsing).

Swift short cycles punctuate the long trends:

cold/warmer   cold/warmer   cold/warmer
sometimes shifting temperatures in two decades

every fifteen hundred years (still shifting).

In Southern California, summer rain stops falling.

Plants and animals move uphill and back down,
          die off, reshape, reappear.

Stressed by altering sea levels and the cycling cold,
        they scatter from one niche to another
        quilting a splendid (still famous) diversity.

                (Southern California boosters will one day brag:
                    ski among pines in the morning
                    lunch among oaks in the afternoon
                    stroll through beach dunes after dinner.
                                  Buy it!)

I MILLION YEARS AGO,
Pacific storms deflect south
        greening Southern California,
            grown cooler, wetter, milder,
      while most of North America dries in the glacial cold.

            Southern California's only glaciers
            crawl down Mt. San Gorgonio
            (Dollar Lake and Dry Lake glacier-carved).

Right here: Winters: warm and wet
                Summers: cool and dry

Los Angeles to Ventura to the Santa Barbara Basin: underwater.

Winter rains rinse down the rising mountains in streams
        carrying dirt, rocks, sand: alluvium
        sliding from the mountain canyons
        into lengthening fans of stream-ruffled sediment
            filling the valleys
                covering the basins

                Stream-layered with alluvium and mountain debris,
        the Simi and San Fernando Valleys
rise above the waterline and slowly dry out.

Los Angeles Basin
San Gabriel Valley
                    linger just underwater.

Pressure from the sliding plates
                              warps and tilts the mountains up
Alluvial dirt rained off the mountains
                              piles up thousands of feet.
The sea covering the old basins,
                    advances and retreats with the cycling cold,
                    grows slowly shallow
                    filled with layer after layer of alluvial silts

And so the ocean begins to recede
and slowly roll back.

730 THOUSAND YEARS AGO
Earth's magnetism fades to nothing (in a day, a week, a thousand years, mystery!)

                              (Every living cell
                                    beneath the magnetic canopy
                                    swept over us from the poles
                              awaits without waiting
                                    for the inevitable
                              weariness of the great magnetic embrace

                                    to soften to fade
                              and leave us all unwrapped,
                              exposed to the cosmic elements)

and revives, enveloping the Earth

          with renewed magnetic poles
          north, once reversed, restored
                    compass pointed to north.

Birds, bees, bacteria, and whales,
guided by the magnetic field,
find their new way.

Near Mammoth Mountain
                              through cracks in the ground
                  red-hot gas explodes magma
                                        so hot it's turned to mineral froth and ash
blasting a hole two miles deep, ten miles wide, twenty miles long
filling with ash, the hole collapses in on itself:
                                        the Long Valley Caldera
                                        (magma still swells beneath Mammoth Mountain)
shock waves shatter the waters of Owens Lake

ash blasts one hundred miles per hour all the way to Kansas

 a meld of thick sizzling layers, rock fragments and ash,
                                        deep-coats the valley for miles

        its age revealed when minerals in the ash cool,
                                                set magnetically north

(so much ash, if it happened here,
it would cover Los Angeles two hundred feet deep).

A condor perched on a rock outcrop in the rising San Gabriels,
        its five-foot black wings folded close by its sides,
                blinks bright yellow eyes,
                        shakes hard, engulfed by a rain of ash.

700 THOUSAND YEARS AGO
More pressure from Baja—caught and dragged northwest by the Pacific Plate—
        (still) jamming Southern California
                against the granite cores of the North American mountain ranges
                (San Bernardinos, Southern Sierra Nevada).

Along the Newport-Inglewood fault
    a line of new hills folds higher:
        Signal, Dominguez, Baldwin, Cheviot

The Santa Susana Mountains crumple east and west
    one side sinks, the other tilts into sharper ridges
    faster than the Santa Clara River can cut through

Blocked, the river bends west along the base of the new mountains
    and empties into the ocean
    through a lush mile-wide delta (Oxnard/Ventura).

From the fast-rising crest of the Santa Susanas and Simi Hills
    rainwater streams southeast into the new San Fernando Valley
    collects in a fresh waterway:

        The Los Angeles River

    meanders
        toward
            the sea.

Rainwater rolling off the Santa Monica Mountains and Simi Hills
    carves a path south (Las Virgenes Canyon)
    and empties into Santa Monica Bay
    shaping the soft expanse of Malibu Lagoon
            (sprawling estates, wet-suited surfers
            snowy egrets, great blue herons
            umbrellas, sand shovels and buckets).

The San Gabriel River, thick with sycamores, willow, blackberry brambles
    rips down the San Gabriel Mountains
        cuts sharp into the rising Puente Hills,
            pushed up along the Puente Hills Fault,

11

The Los Angeles River at Balboa Park: Encino.

notches a gap (Whittier Narrows) to free itself for the sea
    sometimes braids its shallow bed into the course of the Rio Hondo
        ravels loose, and flows south
            through wetland marshes,
                life-filled tide flats (San Pedro Bay) into the Pacific.

What we name Santa Monica and San Pedro Bays round themselves into the landscape
    their edges laced by wetland deltas and seaside lagoons
        where salt tides mingle
            with mountain debris
(mountains given over to sun, wind
            and the rain that washes it all downstream)

                carried in the river waters.

100,000 YEARS AGO
    The world grows colder
    Seawater draws into ice floes
    Icebergs clog the oceans worldwide.

Green and mild Southern California cools.

    Between Barstow and Twentynine Palms
    two volcanoes blow (Amboy and Pisgah:
    youngest so far in Southern California)
    building to black cinder cones
        ash steams into clouds
        lava streams over green fields beside a wide blue lake.

Southern California lush and flourishing:

    Death Valley fills six hundred feet deep with rain and river water:
        Lake Manly
In nearby canyons:
        Lake Tecopa and Panamint Lake
Near Trona:
        Searles Lake

On the road to Las Vegas:
                         Lake Manix
Near Palm Springs in the Salton Trough:
                              Lake Cahuilla fills with Colorado River water.

          Lounging lakeside: wolves, fox, and lions,
          bison and sheep, mammoths and camels
          antelope, horses, and bear

          Feeding in the pluvial waters:
          turtles and snails
          grebes and geese
          cranes, storks, and pelicans

          In pink gusts
                         flamingoes take flight.

The rising San Gabriel mountains look like baby teeth:
sharp and steep
          so steep, they shed rain in slick torrents
          washing thick flows of debris: rock, mud, boulders
          down the waterways and into the valleys,
          century after century,
                         covering the old sea floor (Los Angeles Basin).

Hancock Park lies beneath a blue coastal bay
Its shallowing waters steadily retreating.

75,000 YEARS AGO
Most of the world gripped by harsh, dry cold.
Southern California green and moist.

While the sea recedes and sea level drops (water into ice)
          and the land uplifts
                         ocean waves wear the coast into flatlands

like descending steps
　　　　　　shaping seaside terraces at Vermont and Western.

　　　　　　(In Long Beach near Gaffey Street and the Harbor Freeway)
a gray whale dies and sinks into underwater sands—
　　　　　　　　　　　belly up, head pointed north—
between Palos Verdes Island (we call Peninsula)
and the mainland ten miles away.

Mollusks grip its frame of bones
A harbor seal dies and settles into the frame.

Soon to come, as the sea recedes,
　　　　　　a horse's tooth in a fresh sandy layer
　　　　　　　　　　　and, nearby, bison bones.

50,000 YEARS AGO
　　　　　　The beach is at Baldwin Hills.

The Los Angeles River
　　　　　　flowing since the mountains first rose up,

collects from springs and streams
　　　　　　pouring off the Santa Susana and Santa Monica Mountains and Simi Hills
　　　　　　　　　　　(waters collected from Calabasas and Bell Canyon Creeks
　　　　　　　　　　　begin the river as we know it—striated in concrete)

flows along the base of the Santa Monica Mountains
In later, dryer eras sinks into the valley's soft alluvium, flows underground,
collects in an underground lake,

wells to the surface and swells, stream-fed by a hot spring
　　　　　　　　　　　upwelling in the oak forest (we name Encino—Spanish: oak)
　　　　　　wanders through bulrushes and pond weeds thick in the riverside marshes
　　　　　　　　vibrant with grebes, herons, egrets, swans
　　　　　　　　geese, ducks, and owls
　　　　spreads out after winter rains into flood plains (Balboa Park)
　　　　　　green with elderberry, red cedar, walnut, live oak
its path swathed and softened by wetlands.

grows wide along the way (past Griffith Park)
>joined by large streams from canyons
>in the San Gabriels (Tujunga, Arroyo Seco)
>and from the Verdugo Mountains,
>>through sycamore's wild white branchings and dense willows,
>>vined and brambled with blackberries, raspberries, wild grape
>>tangling over garter snakes, pond turtles, toads, and frogs
>>rainbow trout glisten iridescent, swimming with the chubs and the sticklebacks

breaks toward the coast through a narrow gap
>>between the Elysian and Puente Hills

meanders south, between steep, sycamore and oak forested bluffs
>(we name downtown Los Angeles, Boyle Heights)
>sheltering songbirds, wild turkey, yellow-billed magpies

bends west, beckoned toward the sea
>lolling and shifting in wetland eddies
>channeling a swath (Washington Blvd. and Ballona Creek)

stops at the rising wall of Baldwin, Cheviot, and Beverly Hills
>sprawls into wetlands (La Cienega / The Swamp Blvd.)

collects its forces and cuts the emerging hills

fills with rainwater gathered in creeks
>>flowing down the Santa Monica Mountains
>>(waters now carried in Ballona Creek)
fattens on streams and springs loosed along a ridge
>uplifted by the Santa Monica-Malibu Fault
>(Wilshire Boulevard, Veterans Memorial, University High School)

and empties into the Pacific (Santa Monica Bay).

A luxurious coastal swamp softens the river's flood into the sea
>>a life-rich wet greenery sprawled over two thousand acres

cradled in the Ballona Valley   (Westchester Bluffs to Santa Monica Rise
>Venice, Culver City,
>Marina Del Rey, Playa Del Rey)

12

Snowy egret at the Ballona Wetlands.

its tidal flood, in regular washings,
cleans and nourishes the brackish midlands and salty lowlands where
                      fish spawn and sea otters cavort

on the dry uplands, coyotes range and pronghorn antelope
                      hop through coastal sage, browse among
groves of cypress and Monterey Pine

                              native bees hum past the butterflies
in its border thickets of willow and cottonwoods,
            live oak, alder, walnut, and sycamore

                        birds migrate along the Pacific Flyway
                        in flocks so dense they darken the sky:

        The Ballona Wetlands

                        created by a river: a fifty-two-mile-long river.

                        Smart primates cook supper over fires in Africa,
                        Europe, the Near East, China, Indonesia, Australia,
                        (soon the Americas)
                        bury their dead with banks of flowers,
                        learn to paint with powdered iron,
                        pack stone, bone, antler tool kits,
                        play bone flutes,
                        gather, scavenge, and hunt their food,
                        wear pearly shell, tooth, ivory, carved stone pendants,
                        care for their families.

20,000 YEARS AGO
Maximum worldwide glacial freeze
                        sea level falls hundreds of feet,
                                coastlines fatten.

Cool and wet: winter
        Mild and dry: summer
            Cool and wet: winter
                Mild and dry: summer
                    (Monterey Bay weather in L.A.)

The plentiful winter rains
wash down the mountains in streams
or soak into the loose soil
collecting under Los Angeles
        in underground lakes so full
        their waters would cover one hundred and ten thousand acres
        two hundred feet deep
            (water that pours from our faucets).

Springs brim from the ground, artesian
        (Compton, 1883,
        wells bubbling water into backyards
        capped to stop the flooding).

That old seabed, the Los Angeles Basin

        born of the mountains,
            carried downhill by rivers and streams,
        and the relentless push of the Pacific Plate

        rises above shallowing waters
            and slowly dries out.

Anacapa, Santa Cruz, Santa Rosa, San Miguel,
western peaks of the Santa Monica Mountains,
        lie exposed above the water
            linked as one large island (we name Santarosae).

Plate-pressured uplift and layers of alluvial fans
knit to the mainland

                    hills and mountains
                    that were once islands
                                    (Coyote, Baldwin, Palos Verdes Hills,
                                    Santa Monica Mountains).

Hancock Park, marshy, stream crossed,
slopes gently from the Hollywood Hills.

Amid bustling life in the coastal greens,
black carbon seeps collect in sticky pools
                    (made from the soft inner bodies
                    of minute sea creatures: the diatoms,
                    pressure cooked for ten million years,
                    and heat-risen through fractures and fissures
                    cracked (still cracking) by the Pacific Plate's
                    rough passage northwest)

and the ponded crude oil
            evaporates
                    into thickening films and collecting pits
                            of natural asphalt (La Brea—The Tar Boulevard).

In thousands of moments of staggering surprise,
turtles and spiders, lizards and snails,
wolves, bear, bison, and mammoth,
birds, butterflies, and pill bugs
            mire and die
                    in the relentless, thin layers
                            of leaf and dust covered tar.

The alluvial fans spreading from the mountains
            —stream-etched, softened by springs and swamps—
            meld into verdant coastal plains
                    gray-green sage and pink buckwheat blooms
                    groves of cypress, juniper, and Monterey pine

Close to the mountains, across the inland valleys
                    forests of valley oaks spread their vast arms

Stream-sides thick with sycamore and willow
　　　　　alder and live oak, elderberry and walnut
　　　　　brambles of roses and raspberries

On the mountain slopes
　　　　densely packed, small-leafed, woody bushes
　　　　thrive on lightning fires
　　　　　　　(burned down, they sprout from their root masses;
　　　　　　　 dormant seeds germinate in the heat)
　　　　chemise, Ceanothas (called mountain lilac), manzanita, walnut, pines,
　　　　elderberry and poison oak
　　　　dark green rangy groves of live oak

In the canyons, redwood, bay laurel,
　　　　in springtime dogwood's
　　　　　　　white and pink blossoms glow in the floral profusion

　　　　　　　　　At sunset in Southern California, the spiced air
　　　　　　　　　　　peppery-pungent with the scent of coastal flora

　　　　　　　　Twenty thousand years ago
　　　　　　　　　　　morning glory vines bloom pearl white.

Across Southern California
Meadowlarks and magpies sing in the foliage

Raptors—twenty kinds—circle the skies

California turkeys
Burrowing and night hunting owls
Storks, sandpipers,
Herons, ducks, and geese

Teratorns: fourteen-foot wingspan, thirty-one pounds, short-legged
　　　　stalk turkey chicks, lizards, mice
　　　　　　　small prey trapped in the tar pools
　　　　swallow them whole

Flocks of ravens—those black old birds from Asia—
　　　　yack at their neighbors

13

Pygmy mammoth skull. In the 1930s this skull was collected by the
Santa Barabara Museum of Natural History and is now housed at the
Natural History Museum of Los Angeles. Courtesy of the Vertebrate
Paleontology Collection, Natural History Museum of Los Angeles.

Condors: wattled redheads,
        curious, exuberant social birds, mate for life
        and live for forty years
        carrion eaters with ten-foot wingspans
        already ancient residents of North America—Canada to New York to Texas
        cast shadows (like small aircraft) as they glide
                        across Southern California.

Amid plentiful greens,
plant-eating animals burgeon and bulk:

Slow ambling ground sloths
        six feet tall
Imperial mammoth, grass grazers
        thirteen feet tall at the shoulder
        (leave towering heaps of fertilizing dung)

              good swimmers, some
        cross the Santa Barbara Channel,
        five miles to Santarosae,
        adapting to island life,
        shrink to the size of ponies

Smaller, thick-coated mastodons, six feet at the shoulder,
browse in the (Simi Valley) shrubbery

Native herds of burly, striped horses,
trample the grass by a wide wetland (near Leisure World)

Long-necked llamas and native camels (stroll down Wilshire Boulevard)
wooly bison and mule deer wander over from Asia

Cottontails, jackrabbits
frogs, turtles, toads, and snakes,
bats, mice, and rats

All food for the meat-eating animals
grown huge on a rich diet:

Super-sized jaguar, bobcats, and pumas,
American lions (half a ton, paws the size of dinner plates)
Sabertooth cats with white-knife fangs

Coyote, gray fox,
Timber and dire wolves travel in packs
          scavenge prey caught in the tar pools.

Long-limbed bears with short faces
               tower eleven feet tall on their hind feet
Soon grizzly bear, wandering south through ice openings,
               will arrive and thrive in coastal thickets
                         and eat everything: meat, berries, insects, seeds, and greens.

               In Southern California's cool ice age,
                    plant and animal families
                    couple, birth, grow, die

               Right here — roaring with life.

15,000 YEARS AGO
On the islands and along the broad coast (much wider than the coast we know)
people, in multiple migrations
                    in boats traveling down the coast from Siberia
                    on foot overland through breaks in the ice,
fling fiber nets into the exuberant sea
          gather mollusks from bountiful shores
          (shell mounds grow two stories tall)
harvest and hunt, live and die, among the rich array
naming the new world in ancient languages
                              (lost, evolving,
                              echoing in songs still sung)

With them come their dogs:
          Coyote-sized brown and black Plains dog:
                         household guard, burden carrier
          Small, round, Short-Nosed dog:
                         raised for food
          Small, prick-eared, fox-nosed companion dog,
                    black, black and white, or brown Techichi.

13,000 YEARS AGO

After a short, hard
      millenium of sudden cold
                (a comet shatters over North America?)
      and miles-thick ice sheets
      melting in vast, scouring floods,

across the world
      temperatures rise
                (sea current shifts? sun spots? interglacial mystery)
      heating in abrupt swings.

Sea levels rise hundreds of feet.

                Rains ease off, seasons sharply diverge
         and the vegetation shifts
            diversity narrows as summers lengthen
            plant communities separate into survival zones.

Most huge plant-eating animals,
      the ones whose stomachs
      don't draw nourishment enough
            from sparser feed,
            falter
            generation by generation
            grow fewer, smaller.

In Southern California, warmer, dryer, cycles of drought,
      shorter growing seasons.
           The ancient lakes dry out.

Monterey Bay weather heats to Mediterranean
           (Spanish oranges and olives ripen in future orchards).

All those who have settled here,
      who want to survive the warm resort weather,

have to face the facts:
                    change, move, or die.

Groves of redwood, cypress, and Monterey pine
        the dense, varied, thriving flora
                        dependent on regular and abundant rains   gone.

Grand plant-eating animals
        mammoths, mastadons,
        camels, horses, and ground sloths
                        the ones dependent on ample and easy to digest greens
                        dependent on regular and abundant rains
        (and the scarab beetles—the only local extinct insect—
        dependent on huge piles of mammal dung)

                                                        gone.

Spectacular meat-eating animals
        lions and saber tooth cats,
        huge wolves, towering bears, and multiple raptors
                        dependent on tasty herds of
                        hefty plant-eaters:
                                        completely gone.

But most of them grow smaller, wirier, and stay

        Right here!
                        our home

                        bounded by the bountiful Pacific
                        and angular mountain ranges

                        plate shifting uplifiting earthquaking

                        wet with sloughs and streams
                        renewed with winter river floods and flows

                        sycamore, willow, cottonwood
                        roses and blackberries

                        sages, buckwheat, toyon, tar weed
                        forests of valley and live oak

        Southern California: one of the richest and easiest places to live
                in the whole world.

Right here,
    the people,
   harvesters and hunters,
       stay on and thrive.

9000 YEARS AGO

Among sycamores in Hancock Park, Los Angeles,
  where tar bubbles black
      from ancient layers of a coastal seabed
      through a shifting fabric of earthquake cracks
a family mourns
  the death of a twenty-five-year-old daughter (wife? mother?)

during the annual mourning ceremony
  her bones, gathered from a temporary grave,
    ritually reburied with gifts for her journey:

   shell ornaments
   skull of a Techichi,
    her spirit's guide to the land of souls
   stone mano, purposefully cracked,
      severing ties to the labors of this world
      releasing its spirit for work in the next.

    (We contemplate her body reconstructed
       and named La Brea Woman
   in a museum downhill from the Hollywood sign,
   an exhibit once labeled with a debunked soap opera story
      of murder and a body dumped.)

3000 YEARS AGO

   The Chumash, long settled from San Luis Obispo to Malibu,
    inland to the San Joaquin Valley,
    speak their ancient language,
    trade with their neighbors
      words, goods, marriage partners, rituals.

Waves of new people,

migrating from Northern Mexico (like the land itself)
and south from the Great Basin
arrive in Southern California speaking a language
(we name Uto-Aztecan) they share
with the Aztecs, Hopi, Comanche, and Paiutes.

From the western Santa Monica Mountains to the Santa Susanas to the Salton Sea
the immigrants mingle with those already here
to become the people of this place.

The people name themselves according to where they live.

Among the many tribes are those who (now) call themselves:
Tongva, Acjachemen, Quechnajuichom.

(The Spanish will name them after their missions:
Gabrielino, Juaneño, Luiseño).

At home in hundreds of communities, the people
weave large houses (some are like baskets overturned)
bathe daily before sunrise in spring-fed pools
eat breakfast with their families.

A few of their many villages:

On a broad coastal terrace spreading seaward
at the foot of the Santa Monica Mountains
on the Chumash-Tongva border
beside a rippling lagoon
where Malibu Creek empties into the bay:
Humaliwo: "Place Where the Surf Sounds Loudly"

Perfectly located on a sunny expanse
beside a large year-round creek
in the Santa Monica Mountains
with marine, canyon, and upland forage:
Topanga: "Village Where the Mountains Run Out to the Sea"

14

Point Dume, shrine and burial site: Malibu.

In a city the Spanish will name "live oak": Encino
beneath a live oak canopy
beside a warm spring flowing into a wetland
emptying into the Los Angeles River:
Siutcanga: "Village Among the Oaks"

At the mouth of Little Tujunga Canyon
where ample waters flow into
a wide valley, and where, in a red rock cliff
the image of an old capitana, tuxuu'
sits on her knees, looking south:
Tujunga: "Village of the Old Woman"

In West Los Angeles at University High School,
fast-flowing springs, set free by the fault uplift,
spread into verdant and bird-happy marshes
before pouring downhill to the Ballona Wetlands:
Koruuvanga: "Village Where We Are In the Sun"

A regional center with a vast cemetery
along bluffs above the floodplain
and at the base of the bluffs,
beside an ample and verdant wetland,
named Ballona after Rancho de Ballona:
Washna

Near Studio City, at the base of green hills,
where nearby a large stream, flowing out of a canyon
named Tujunga
braids into the Los Angeles River:
Cahuenga: "Village Near the Mountain"

At the intersection of Forest Lawn
and Crystal Springs Drive, between the
mountains of Griffith Park
and the verdant banks of the Los Angeles River:
Hahamonga: "Walking, They Seated Themselves"

Downtown Los Angeles,
near City Hall and Union Station,
among dense sycamores, alder, willow,
and hillsides flush with wild roses
beside the Los Angeles River:
Yanga: "Place Where the Earth is Salty"

In the San Gabriels at Chileao Flats,
among pines and granite outcrops
home of royal clans of the
mountain-loving people
including the woman shaman Toypurina:
Hapchinga

In open country near the Dominguez Hills
between Watts, Lynwood, and Compton,
beside an old spring and willow forest,
land that became Rancho Tajuata—
its name formed from the Tongva village:
Huutnga: "Village in the Willows"

In Long Beach, on the university campus,
by a willow-thick stream, amid cottonwood forests,
a birthplace of the great Wiyot,
and the hilltop birthplace
of the creator spirit, Chinigchinich:
Povunga: "Village Within a Stone Sphere" or "The Gathering Place"

Near Mission San Juan Capistrano
amid a forest of valley oaks
home of the beloved woman chief, Coronne,
the Mother Village of the Acjachemen
whom the Spanish will name the Juaneños:
Putiidhem: "The Navel"

Close by the city of Temecula,
ancestral village of the Pechaa'ang,

one group of the Quechnajuichom
whom the Spanish will name the Luiseños
after their mission: San Luis Rey de Francia:
Temeekunga: "The Place of the Sun"

In the San Gorgonio Pass near Palm Springs,
at the mouth of Whitewater Canyon
near a seasonal river, brilliant
with wildflowers in springtime:
Wanup

Recognizing the Ancestors in the land's power and presence
the people name every curve and lift,
every plant and animal,
every boulder, creek, spring, and mountain
according to its nature.

(They read the landscape like we read a book.)

Life, right here, unfolds for many thousands of years,
within the sacred circle of First People:

Kas'élewun: "Place of the Tongue"   Castle Peak in the Simi Hills

'Iwihinmu: "Mystery"   Mount Pinos and Mount Frazier in the
and Toshololo   San Emigdio Mountains
(the center of the world
lies between them in
the Cuddy Valley)

Hidakupa: "The Mountain Was Standing"   San Gabriel Mountains

Juit gait: "Snow Mountain" (home of *pah'ah*, the bighorn sheep) — Mount San Antonio, "Old Baldy," in the San Gabriel Mountains

Piwipwi: "Bear Mountain / Gray Back" — Mount San Gorgonio in the San Bernardino Mountains

Jamiwo: (home of the cannibal Takwish) — Mount San Jacinto in the San Jacinto Mountains

Xuungova near the village of Paama'yam: "White-headed Eagle" — Santiago Peak (Kalaupa) and Modjeska Peak: Saddleback in the Santa Ana Mountains

Pimu — Catalina Island

Sumo: The sea-goer's name for the village of "Abundance" — Paradise Cove near Point Dume: Santa Monica Bay

Asawtnga: "Mountain of the Eagle" — Saddle Peak in the Santa Monica Mountains

Gazing to the north
      east
         south
           west
             and to the center

the landscape is completely familiar.

Named, it is home.
      Singing its story, the land abides.

Book Two ❧ INDIGENOUS MYTHS AND SONGS

1   *Universe, World, People*

First

there is

quiet.

Only solitude

like an empty house   (no house)

Only

Kvish Atakvish

Kvish: Empty

Atakvish: Vacant

These two are man and woman, brother and sister.

Then Kvish Atakvish

becomes

Omai Yamai

Omai: Not Alive

Yamai: Not in Existence

When these two discover themselves,
they talk with one another:

Brother, who are you?

Sister, who are you?

(Desire stirs the man,
so he never again calls her sister.)

She asks again: Who are you?

He says:

Kvish

Kvish

Kvish

I am   Empty

Empty

Empty

He blows out his spirit breath: Hannnn!

She answers:

Atakvish

Atakvish

Atakvish

I am   Vacant

Vacant

Vacant

She blows out her spirit breath: Hannnn!

She asks again: Who are you?

He answers:

    Omai

    Omai

    Omai

                I am   Not Alive

                         Not Alive

                         Not Alive

He blows out his spirit breath: Hannnn!

He asks again: Who are you?

She answers:

    Yamai

    Yamai

    Yamai

                 I am   Not in Existence

                         Not in Existence

                         Not in Existence

She blows out her spirit breath: Hannnn!

        Not Alive-Not in Existence

            becomes

        Whaikut Piwkut Harurai Chatuta

Whaikut Piwkut: Pale Gray   The Milky Way

Harurai Chatutai: Changing   Descending Deep into the Heart

These two become

Tukmit: Dark Sky   Tomaiyowit: Earth

(Clearly it is not
        male and female
        sky and earth,
                but of another nature.)

These two:

Tukmit   Tomaiyowit   Dark Sky   Earth

        come forth from what came before
        not as children
        but as themselves:
                        a Continuing Being.

It is very dark
                without stars, sun, moon.

The woman lies with her feet to the north.

The man sits by her right side.

In the darkness
        they talk with one another again,
        and what they name
        they become:

                The First World.

He asks: Who are you?

She answers: I am Tamaiyowit.

She asks: Who are you?

He answers: I am Tukmit.

Tamaiyowit speaks again:
> I am Earth
> I stretch to the horizon
> I quake
> I shake
> I rumble
> I am round
> I revolve
> I roll out of sight and return.

Tukmit speaks again:
> I am Dark Sky
> I rise
> I arch
> I cover
> I come from the east
> I devour all in one bite
> I seize and send away human spirits
> I sever
> I am death.

Sitting by her side in the darkness
> Tukmit feels Tamaiyowit's right hand.

He asks: What is this?
She answers: My right hand.

> Tukmit finds Tamaiyowit's left hand.

He asks: What is this?
She answers: My left hand.

15

Hand petroglyph near a Tataviam village: Vasquez Rocks.

He touches her head and asks: What is this?
>   She answers: My hair.

Feeling each part of her body,
>   he asks again and again: What is this?

>   She answers: My hair parting
>   My skull
>   My temple
>   My forehead
>   My ears
>   My brow
>   My eyebrows
>   My eyelids
>   My cheekbones
>   My nose
>   My lips
>   My mouth
>   My tongue and palate
>   My teeth, front teeth and eye teeth
>   My chin
>   My neck

Moving his hand down the length of her body,
>   Tukmit continues asking,
>   asking and touching
>   Tamaiyowit answers him,
>   naming and becoming.

He sighs
She resists, reminding him
>   that she is his sister,
>   but they continue
>   until, finally, they are united.

She is pregnant.

Tamaiyowit grows so large,
     when she sits down to rest.
       she falls over backward.

Groaning, she looks around for help.

Tukmit relieves her with his sacred *paviut*:
         his flint tipped wand

He cuts her from the breastbone down

Groaning, he cuts her open to deliver her.

Groaning, she bears
    The First People:

        Spirit and Hair   (hair, where the spirit resides)

        Rush Basket and Curved Throwing Stick
            (basket protecting girls' faces
            during their initiation)

        Iron Scum   (bubbling from springs, to be burned and mixed for
            the ground painting after the girls' initiation)
        and

        Green Scum   (algae blooming in springs
            when Tamaiyowit has her menses)

        Water and Mud

        Wild Roses and Blackberries
            (thorny avengers of the spirit-to-come:
            Chinigchinich)

        Mountain Tussock Grass and Wetland Sedge
            (grasses for lining the steam pit and for covering the
            girls during initiation)

        Salt Grass and Ordinary Grass

        Bleeding and First Menses

            These are the First Born.

Then Tamaiyowit bears the hills, trees, stones, rocks,
(everything we see on Earth).

All of these are also First People.
Intelligent beings charged with power.

Then she gives birth to:

Badger
Buzzard, who is the star Altair
Spirit Lightning, the feared Takwish
Growling Subterranean Water Monster, Choruwut
The Spirit of People that Survives the Corpse
Black Oak with Acorns
Cottonwood Box for Sacred Feathers
Mourning Pole, the Kutumit, and Baskets Hung on It
Mountain Ash Tree
Wild Cherry Tree
Large Brake Fern

Then she gives birth to those who will be messengers and avengers
of the spirit-to-come, Chinigchinich

Among them are:
Black Rattlesnake
Red Rattlesnake
Spider
Tarantula Hawk
Raven
Bear
Stingray

Then she gives birth to the ceremonial tools:

Tukmul: Flat Winnowing Basket where ritual offerings,
grains and sacred pipes, are placed

Somkul Papawish: Urine and the Mock Orange branch for sprinkling it over
offerings during boys' initiation

Topal Tamyush: Stone Mortar for grinding seeds and roots and the sacred
                    Stone Mortar for grinding Datura, called
                    Manit, The Vine That Can Talk,
                    to be drunk by doctors
                    and given to boys who dream their guardian spirits
                    during initiation.

All of these are also First People.

Next Tukmit and Tamaiyowit create the land.

The way people around San Juan Capistrano say it,
        at first it's a small place
                    but they expand it
                            until it's as wide as it is today.
The salty and bitter ocean is Tamaiyowit's urine.

People from around Los Angeles say it this way:
            The new land is placed on the shoulders
                    of six Great Beings.
        Among them are:
                Eagle (who is Wiyot, great captain of the First People)
                Datura (the Great Woman, Giver of Visions)
                Breath of Life
                Sun Captain
                Deer who is Earth, Mother of All Beings

Whenever these Great Beings
            turn or stretch
                    the Earth quakes.

Others who live around Ventura say
            at the very bottom
                    coil

two gigantic water snakes
who hear the doctor's singing.
Whenever the snakes move,
the earth quakes.

Still other people who live near the coast say that Dark Sky
shaped the Earth as a sphere that he holds in his hands.

But the sphere won't stop moving,
so he steadies it by placing in its center
a *toshaawt*:
a powerful black stone.

A small stream of water,
miserably crowded with Fish People,
circles the earth.

One day, unable to suffer any longer,
the Fish People gather in a council
to discuss their desperate situation.
Should they stay in the water
or crawl out onto the land
even though they have no legs or feet?
While they debate, a giant fish arrives
carrying a *toshaawt*.

Cracking open the stone, they discover a bladder filled with gall.

When they empty the gall into the stream,
fresh water turns salty and bitter,
and the waters expand
flowing over the earth
filling the oceans
just as they are today.

Now everything has taken shape
just as Tukmit and Tamaiyowit
named
in their conversation.

Still, there is no light at all.

In the darkness,
     in the far north,
          the First People cannot see
          but only feel one another.

          So they travel east
            until they are stopped,
               (near San Bernardino) by Growing Darkness
                 like a hill they cannot climb over
                 like a blank wall.

They can go no farther.

          They turn around
        and return
     to the place where they started.

Then the First People come upon a canyon
          so narrow they cannot get through.

Then they come to a resting place (near Elsinore),
          stop, and create a lake there.

Then they travel to Echva Temeko (Temecula),
          and rest by a small lake.

This is where the First People become conscious beings.

     They begin to think.
     They begin talking with one another.
     They begin asking one another: What should we do now?

Hainit Yunenkit Headband to Hold Eagle Down Feathers   Deep Underground Diver
          decides to create Temet, the sun,
               and set him into the sky.

After he makes the sun, he gathers milkweed and twists the reddish fibers into twine.
From the twine, he weaves a very large, long net.

Hainit Yunenkit calls everyone to Temecula where they gather in a council.

(Rocks and trees still sit in a circle there.
Stones lean together in groups of three
where they were used to cook food.
Piles of ash are still there.)

With groans and cries,
he rolls up his net,
and lays it on the ground in front of the People.

Singing to Temet, they spread out the huge net and place him in it.

With groans and cries:
Temet Kwon na num
Temet Kwon na num
Temet Kwon na num

And blowing their spirit breath to the sky: Han-han-n han-n-n!

they raise the net
slinging him into the sky as the sun.

The sun flies north,
but that isn't the right place,
and he returns.

They put Temet back in the net.
With groans and cries and chanting again,
they raise the net
slinging him into the sky.

But he would not fly south,
and returns.

They put Temet back in the net.
With groans and cries and chanting again,
they raise the net
slinging him into the sky.

Temet flies a little way west
　　　　　　　and comes down again.

They put Temet back in the net.
With groans and cries and chanting again,
　　　　　　　they raise the net
　　　slinging him into the sky.

They send him way off to the east
　　　　　　　where he settles.

They blow out their spirit breath to him:
　　　　　　　Han-n-n, wahha, wahha, wah-ha-a!

Gazing across a great distance, they seek their son
　　　　From far away they seek him
　　　　From far away they seek him
　　　From a sandy place near Temecula.

Gazing across a great distance, they look for him
Across a great distance, searching for their son.

We all saw him in the east
We all found him.
The sun was there in the east.

In the east, Black Swift saw him.
In the east, Hawk saw him.
In the east, Kingbird and Coyote saw him.
In the east we saw him.
　　　　　　　We all found him there.
In the east there it was, the sun.
In the east, we found him.
　　　　　　　We saw him.

The sun rises high overhead.

Light shines on the First People.

16

Summer Solstice ceremonial site. In the distance is the hooked stone that,
with the rising sun behind it, casts a shadow across the cupoled rock and
nearby bear paw: Simi Hills.

The sun is rising!
The sun is rising!

The sun is rising!
The sun is rising!

They are filled with joy! They can see one another!

The clever way the First People flung Temet—
    criss-crossing his tracks—
            he could not follow the same path across the sky
                but would work his way north and south
                    with the seasons.

                (Celebrations mark the Winter Solstice,
                when Temet arrives and stays
                five days at his southern house.

                When he leaves to start his new rounds,
                    everyone rejoices.)

Now there are three layers:

In the world above: Sun and other Sky People
In the middle: People of the world-becoming
In the world below: monsters, water snakes, and other dangerous spirit beings.

At this time the First People speak only one language.

Tukmit says to his children:

        "Some of you must travel north, some east, some south, some west."

As they go, he gives them their religion and their new languages.

          (He left us with our language,

             right here,

                in the center.)

Now all things are ready.

Tamaiyowit lies resting, outstretched,

    her feet to the north   her head to the south

    her left hand to the west   her right hand to the east.

The First World, once noisy and disturbed, is calm and quiet.

2 ❧ *The Great Captain Wiyot:*
Death, Spirit, Power

As they were traveling from the north,
the First People were lead by Wiyot, a brilliant captain,
the last born of Tukmit and Tamaiyowit.

Though all of the First People had their own indestructible, beneficial, dangerous
ayelkwi: knowledge that creates power,

Wiyot's knowledge-power, was greatest of all the People.
He knew everything.

A wise and generous teacher, everyone called him Father,
though they were not born to him.

One day, the First People stopped by a pond to swim and rest.
Among them was Red-legged Frog, Wahawut,
a woman with big eyes and nice shoulders.

When the other People jumped into the water, she sat still on the bank with her glossy long
hair falling all the way over her hips.

Wiyot couldn't take his eyes off her, and he was all swelled up.
Wahawut noticed his condition and at the same time, with her power, read his mind.

When she finally leaped into the water with her long, shapely legs, her hair flew way up,
and Wiyot saw her thin, boney frog back and hips.

Wahawut instantly knew when his desire turned to disgust.

She grew very angry.

She summoned the People who lived underground and underwater:
Pocket Gopher
Meadow Mouse
Angleworm

After she told them about the insult, they determined to kill Wiyot.

As soon as they started working, he grew sick.

This happened in April: The Green Grass month, the month of rains.

Now the spider web
    catches
        butterflies
        grasshoppers.

The way some people around San Juan Capistrano say it,
    when Wiyot grew old, he became weak and cruel,
        so his sons decided to kill him.
    They handed him a poisoned drink
        and he became immediately sick.

His mother, knowing her son was in danger,
    prepared a remedy.
In an abalone shell, she mixed her urine
    with certain herbs
    and set it in the sun to cook.

But Coyote came along and accidentally
    gave the shell
        a kick,
      spilling all the medicine.
Now there was no medicine
    powerful enough to save Wiyot.

Wiyot called together his People.
    They were all doctors.
    Just by looking at him, they would know what was wrong.

People came from the north: the Tamyush, Sacred Stone Mortars for grinding datura root,
    came walking along, swinging from rim to rim.
People came from the east: the stars Nükülish (Antares) and Yungavish (Altair).

People came from the south: the Tule and the Pine Tree People.
People came from the west: the Valley Oak and Live Oak People.

But no one knew the poison. No one could cure him.

Other doctors: Tarantula Wasp
                  Burrowing Owl
                  Hummingbird
                              tried their powers to cure him.

But Wiyot grew worse. He was paralyzed, couldn't walk, and had to crawl around.

When it was Titmouse's turn to try, he laid his ear over Wiyot's chest
                  and listened deeply
                              to his heart and breath.

That's how he learned that it was Wahawut's power that was killing Wiyot.

But no one could find Wahawut. She had disappeared into mud and water.

Wiyot realized how sick he was.

He asked his People to take him to hot springs in the Cahuilla Valley.
Here he rested and lay in the healing waters.
But he grew worse.

The People took him to Warner Hot Springs.
He only grew worse and could no longer walk.

The People moved him in a carrying net
        to San Jose Hot Springs in the Warner's Ranch Valley.
Here he grew even worse.

The People carried him to Agua Tibia Hot Springs where he grew weaker.

The People carried him to Murrieta Hot Springs where he grew weaker yet.

The People carried him to Elsinore Hot Springs.

It was no use. Wiyot could barely talk.

Lying close to death, Wiyot confided in Kingbird,
      a good man who stayed close by his side.
He told Kingbird about what would happen in the future
      and how to keep the world in balance.

He told Kingbird he would die very soon,
      but that after this happened, he would return in three days.
Only Kingbird would see him in the east
      where he would rise as Moila, the moon.

Gathering all the other People close around him,
      Wiyot spoke about the races they would run
          when a new moon rose.
After he died, he said, they would see him in the west.

Wiyot told them: "I think I shall die soon."

He recited the months, the Moon Names, when he might die,
      saying each time, "Perhaps I will die in this one."

          The calendar unfolded as he spoke
      with seasons, new and full moons, stars rising and setting.

As each month passed, the First People waited.

He lived through April, the Little Big Month when the rains come;
      the Green Grass month when grasses sprout.

He lived through May, The Big Big Month.

He lived through June, the Little Month of bright summer air,
      when the young eagles fly.

He lived through July, the Big Month of bright summer air,
      when the Pleiades rise,
      marking the center of summer.

He lived through August, the Little Month when things turn brown and dry,
      when the stars of Orion's Belt rise,
      marking the turn toward winter.

He lived through September, the Big Month when grass and leaves wither.

He lived through October, the Little Wind Whistling Month,
                    when winds sweep through branches,
                    when rivulets wash the fallen leaves.

He lived through November, The Big Wind Whistling Month.

He lived through December, The Little Fat Padded Month,
                    when deer fatten,
                    bears fatten and shed their fur,
                    and the whales fatten.

He lived through January, The Big Fat Padded Month,
                    when Antares rises,
                    marking the first turn toward spring.

He lived through February, The Little Tree Sprouting Month,
                    when frogs sing,
                    snakes emerge,
                    trees are wet with sap and thick with buds;
                    when Altair, the Buzzard, rises
                    marking the turn toward spring.

He lived through March, The Big Tree Sprouting Month.

He lived through April, the second year of his sickness.
                    He renamed it: The Little Green Grass Month
                    That Repeats Itself.

He lived through May and renamed it The Big Big Month That Repeats Itself.

Wiyot, suffering and weak but alive,
          lived until June-July, a double month, which he renamed:
                    Little Month of Taking All Into the Mouth
                    Big Month of Taking All Into the Mouth.

Now he spoke his final words:
                    "Into my mouth I take
                      all living things,
                        the whole world,
                    I take them with me into death."

Some people say Wiyot died at Elsinore Hot Springs.
Others say Wiyot died near Temecula.
And some say he died in the mountains
near Big Bear Lake
or near Mt. San Gorgonio: Piwipwi, Great Grayback,
the Granite Gleaming Mountain.
His cremation created its
red, black, and white earth.

Another way people say it, is that he died where he was born:
at the village of Povunga, in Long Beach,
by a large spring and cottonwood forest.

When Wiyot died, his great *ayelkwi*, knowledge-power,
scattered throughout the world,
though it settled unevenly—

more here
less there—
a residue of intelligence and will in First People everywhere:
Plant and Animal People
Mineral, Weather, and Water People
Basket, Net, Pipe, and Mortar People
People of the World Above
People of the World Below.

(Doctors of the people-to-come
will seek to add new *ayelkwi*
to the powers with which they are born.

And so they carefully study and test the power
of everything around them.

A doctor who wants to take on
an object's or an animal's power
must learn its language.

The more knowledge doctors gain,
the more languages they speak,
the more power and respect
they gather to themselves.

Gaining power is very dangerous.
Each new power must be studied and practiced
strictly according to its nature.
Otherwise, starvation, drought,
disease, and death might be released
on the doctor and on the people.)

The First People gathered in a council to talk over what they should do:
burn Wiyot's body or bury him.

They decided to burn him.

Kangaroo Rat got right to work.
From Milkweed he made twine and wove a carrying net to lift Wiyot's body.

Old Woman Glow-worm kept fire hidden carefully under her arm.

The rest of the People dug a shallow hole and heaped it with firewood.

While the People were busy making preparations, they kept an eye on Coyote.

Blow Fly and Coyote were hovering around Wiyot during his last days,
drinking his tears.
Were they caring for Wiyot,
or were they vying for who would light the pyre?

The People were suspicious of them both, but especially of Coyote.

Coyote was often mean and nobody trusted him.
They decided to send him away while they burned the body.

To get his attention, the People flattered Coyote.
They told him he was the only one who could fetch fire
because he had the power to make distance shorter
by drawing the earth together with two of his hands.

They told him he was the fastest of all, so of course he was the only one
who should race north to bring back fire.

"Go all the way," they said, "Don't stop until you get there."

Coyote didn't want to leave.
When he headed toward the First People in the north,
    he only ran a short way,
    turned around, and loped back
    saying he couldn't get any fire there.

So they sent him to the First People in the west.
He went a little farther but raced back,
    saying he couldn't get any fire there.

They sent him to the First People in the south and in the east.
Each time he went a little farther but raced back
    saying he couldn't get any fire there.

While Coyote was away, Wiskun, Chipmunk, using his power,
    carried a log so heavy
            ten men couldn't move it.
  At first, he couldn't even push it with his foot.

Then he turned all the way around once,
    calling to the north, east, south, west, and center.
After he did this, he rolled it along the ground like a stick,
     and finally carried it to where Wiyot lay.

When he put it down, the People asked, "What happened to that huge log?
        This looks to us like a small stick!"
This log became the first *mavakal*.

Staggering under his load, Kangaroo Rat used his net
    to lift Wiyot's body onto the half-hollowed out log, the *mavakal*,
    and laid him out.

   (Kangaroo Rat still has those net marks on his forehead and back.)

As was the custom of the First People, Wiyot wore no clothes.
On his breast they laid the beaded feather-skin of the Raven.

They covered Wiyot's body using the other half of the hollowed log, the *avakal*,

circled the pyre three times,
and stood facing the sacred north.

It was Glow-worm who lighted Wiyot's pyre,
although some people say it was Blow Fly
who did it using her fire sticks.

(That's why the fly still rubs her legs together.)

As the fire burned, all the People,
the Animal and Plant People,
the Pine Trees and Cottonwoods,
Willows, Cedar, and Spruce,
gathered in a close circle around Wiyot's pyre
to prevent Coyote from reaching the body.

When Coyote saw the black smoke curling in air, he came racing back, crying:
"Why did you fool me? I've got to see my father!"

Coyote, Coyote
wandering around here crying
Coyote, Coyote
wandering around here crying

Wandering around here
crying and trembling
Wandering around here
crying and trembling

Coyote Coyote
wandering around here crying
Wandering around here
crying and trembling

His gray hair turns whiter
wandering around here crying
Turns whiter
wandering around here crying

Coyote, Coyote crying,
trembling and crying.

17

Winter Solstice petroglyph detail possibly depicting Coyote among other images: Simi Hills.

Coyote circled the People,
       peering over their heads,
              calculating how he would get to Wiyot.

Moving back so he would have a running start, he leaped
       over Badger, the shortest man in the circle,
                    and jumped into the pyre.

       Coyote seized Wiyot's heart, jumped back over Badger, and ran.

Some of the People ran after him, clubbing Coyote
       with the pokers they used to stir up the fire.

          (Coyote still has those ragged black marks on his back.)

Coyote raced far ahead of the People, stopped, and ate Wiyot's heart.

          (That's why, when an important captain or doctor dies,
          before his cremation, a ceremony leader
          eats a piece of his flesh, just as Coyote did.)

         It was complete and nothing could change it.

         Death would stay in the world.

The People returned and tended the fire until nothing was left but the bones.

                  Wiyot's white ashes
                  He is embers, he is embers
                  He is embers
                  He is embers.

Deeply moved by their grief, some Bird People rolled around the fire weeping.

Valley Quail, Mountain Quail, Red-shafted Flicker, and Roadrunner
       mourned so deeply,
              they decided to cut their hair.

(That is why these birds have bobbed topknots.
And that is why, when a leader
or close family member dies,
people cut their hair.)

Brush Rabbit, Toovit,
              holding the first instrument,
                    a doctor's rattle
              made with the long cocoons of the Ceanothus moth,

                          stood up and sang.

He was no longer an ordinary man.
He was the First Singer
              a Singing Man

                    a Man of Power.

                          (He began the song cycle
                          still sung at the mourning ceremonies.)

Toovit's singing inspired Sandhill Crane and Crow to start dancing
                          (though some say it was Cricket).
              Surprised by how funny they looked,
                    for a moment the People forgot their grief,
                          and laughed.

                          (At the mourning ceremonies,
                          people repeat the laughing sounds
                          Sandhill Crane made as he danced.)

When the funeral pyre died down, the People gathered Wiyot's bones.
Sitting together in a council, they discussed what to do with them.

While they talked, Eagle,
                    a wise man with great *ayelkwi*,
              understood what it meant that death was in the world.

He decided to find out if there was any way to avoid it.

With his great power, he was sure he could fly to the very limits and escape.

> When Eagle flew north, he found death.
> When Eagle flew east, he found death.
> When Eagle flew south, he found death.
> When Eagle flew west, he found death.

Seeing death everywhere, he returned to the center and accepted future-fate:
he would allow himself as a fledgling
    to be captured,
        lovingly tended,
          danced,
            killed without his blood being shed,
and mourned for three days and nights.

For all time there is only one Eagle.

(Doctors wear his feathers in their headdresses.
Whirling dancers wear his feathers
    in their ceremonial skirts to honor his power
    to increase fertility and longevity.)

Beneath the sacred milkweed string,
    the Milky Way,
Lie down alone
    Follow me, catch me
Feather headdress
    Follow me, catch me
Beneath the feather headdress
    Sun, Eagle, my Brother.

Gathering the People, Eagle announced:
"Death is everywhere.
Death is always close by.
Death is inescapable."

They would have to die, all of them.

When it was time to die,
   when I learned about death,
My heart was surprised.
Everything failed me.
I was sad to leave my home.
I gazed far-off and
   sent my spirit
      north, east, south, west
       to escape death.
But I found nothing.
There was no escape.

As Eagle grew sick, he talked to the People about their spirits,
   telling them that their hearts are the center
   and that the breath of life lives there.

When death comes,
   early in the morning
      when it is not yet light,
  the spirit flies over a great sea
     to a gate in the east.
Here it enters the Other World,
   the Above and Below,
  to shine as a new star in Towish,
     the Milky Way.

Some people around San Pedro and Los Angeles
  say the spirit
   flies west over Pimu, Catalina Island,
  to live well in the Other World,
    the Above and Below.
Only great captains and doctors shine in the Milky Way.

In the morning, in the morning,

Floating here, floating here

In the morning, in the morning.

The gray gleam of Towish reminds us
we are only going to live here for a little while.

(When people die,
their hearts are tied into the four corners of the sky,
held by Wanawu—one of the First People—
the sacred string net
that is Towish, the Milky Way.

This is how they settle into the Other World
and can't return,
freed from the middle world of the living.)

My heart goes crying,
crying crying.
My heart goes crying.

The body is lost.
The body is gone.

My heart goes crying,
crying, crying.
My heart goes crying.

After he died, the People heard something far away.

It was Eagle's spirit singing.

3   *Food, Feasting, Deer, Moon*

With the death of Wiyot, the world stopped expanding to hold more People,
and white clay, their only food, no longer nourished them.

The First People began thinking about the ceremonies
        they must now perform,
                and they realized that ceremonies
                        require feasting.
Since they could no longer eat white clay,
        their need to eat
        left only once choice:
                they must eat each other.

That's when they confronted Deer.

The People told him they wanted to kill and eat him.
But Deer argued, "No, that's not right. I'm no different than you are.
        I know what you know."

The People offered to kill him using sacred stones.
        In front of him they lined up huge white crystals.
But Deer said: "No, I have those, too. My fat looks just like that."

The People said they had feathers that could kill him.
Deer said, "No, I have hair like that."

They said they would kill him with sinew.
But Deer said, "No, I have sinew, too."

They said they would kill him with blood.
Deer said, "No, I have blood, too."

They said they would kill him with foot tracks.
But Deer said, "No, some of those tracks are mine."

They told him they would kill him with marrow, ears, eyes.
But Deer said, "No, I have all those things, too."

FOOD, FEASTING, DEER, MOON

They said they would kill him with the deer head
                    they would use in hunting to deceive the game.
But Deer said, "No, I have one of those."

They told him they would kill him with tobacco, but Deer said he had some.

They told him they would kill him with ticks, but Deer said he had ticks.

They told him they would kill him with blue flies, but Deer said he had those, too.

When the People laid down in front of him flint tipped arrows
            winged with feathers that would fly after him,
                    Deer gave up.
                                He didn't know about this.
                                He had no more to say.

They killed him with their bows and arrows and skinned him—
                though some say it was Blue Fly
                and others say it was Mountain Lion who killed him.
They saved his legs bones for awls to use for making baskets.

These they gave to Katydid, Shulkul, who was the first woman to make a basket. Katydid
        wasted no time weaving a large one to hold Wiyot's bones.

        Some people say Wahawut, Red-legged Frog
        —but not the one who killed Wiyot—wove the first basket.

The People, after deciding who was to eat whom,
                just as they had decided who would live where—
                    in the ground, in the trees, in the water, in the air—
killed other People for food, too, like Rabbit, Acorn,
                and many other animals, seeds, fruits, and plants.

                    (This is why people hold ceremonies
                        for harvesting and hunting.)

Deer hunters always gather to sing and dance
the night before setting out.

Their songs increase and attract
                                    the animals they seek
                    in the same way doctors sing up the rain.

Spirits who see us
            spirits, spirits, spirits, spirits, spirits
They're calling me
            spirits, spirits
They're guiding me
            spirits, spirits,
They're calling me
            spirits, spirits
                        They're guiding me.

The hunter sings about when he will first see a deer.

I walk and sing.
I say to myself, walking and singing,
            I say to myself, walk toward it quietly.

Quietly I'm walking and singing.
I say to myself, walk toward it quietly,
            Sing and walk quietly.

When he calls the deer, it comes toward him.

Are you keeping your heart in the mountain brush?
Are you keeping your heart in the mountain brush?

My hand disappears in a smoky haze
My power reaches from my hand
            to his heart in the mountain brush.

When the hunter cries out, the deer falls down,
                        and he cuts its throat.

Great Grandfather Green Fly motions to the hunter
            and he follows
                        to where the deer lies.

He tells you, he tells me
Great Grandfather Green Fly

                    Green Fly

                    Green Fly
He sends you hints, he sends me hints

My Great Grandfather Green Fly
My Great Grandfather Green Fly

He tells you, he tells me.

To honor his bond
                    with Deer's spirit.
a hunter never eats
                    the one he kills.

Hunting this way, there is always plenty of meat.

When the People finished their council, they knew what to do with Wiyot's bones.

Using Katydid's basket, they carried them to a stone mortar
          where they were ground and mixed with water into mush.
They dug a small pit, poured in the mixture,
                    and covered it carefully.

     With their breath, groaning and chanting
                    to the north, east, south, west, and center,
          they sent Wiyot's spirit to the Milky Way.

(Like Wiyot, each person's spirit
                    has its own *ayelkwi*
freed by death from the world of the living.

Burning images and possessions of the dead,
and other ceremonies they did for Wiyot
               protect the living
                    by sending the spirits of the dead to Towish.)

18
Memorial pole and view of the
village of Povunga: Long Beach.

Noise echoed in my little house.
Now my house is deserted.
The echoing sound has deserted
                              my little house.

Noise echoed in my little place
                              here in my little place.
Noise echoed here, in this, my little place.
A little noise echoed here.

Noise echoed in my little house.
The echoing has deserted it
Deserted this, my dwelling place.

Noise echoed in my little house.
The echoing sound has deserted it.

Eastward it went.
Eastward it went.
Eastward it went.
Eastward it went
                    rumbling like an earthquake.

Moving forever eastward
Climbing forever eastward
Traveling forever eastward
Going forever toward the dawn.

Three days after Wiyot died, Kingbird flew to his housetop,
          though some people say he flew
            to the highest mountain, Piwipwi, Mt. San Gorgonio,
      where he announced to the People that Wiyot was coming.

          (Even today, early in the morning,
                you can hear him singing:
                    "Wiyot is coming! Wiyot is coming!")

The People immediately gathered to look for Wiyot,
          but only Kingbird saw him in the morning,
                rising in the east as the new moon, Moila.

Moila traveled across the sky to the west where Coyote saw him and cried out:
"Moila has come!" Then all the People saw him, too,
a moon sliver so thin that at first he was barely visible.

Seeing Moila, the People, exhaling loudly,
blowing their spirit breaths to him
exclaiming three times,
Hannn! Hannn! Hannn!

(Captains and doctors, who know
when the new moon will rise, watch for it.
They gather the people and prepare a fire.

When the moon appears on the horizon,
they light the fire with their long, ceremonial pipes
and all cry out to Moila,
just as the First People did.

Then the people race in a line, side by side,
until the fastest runner passes ahead
and all return to the fire where they started.

If there is an eclipe, it is Wiyot's sickness
during the months before he died.
When the moon clears,
Wiyot as Moila becomes well again.

Everything works according to the moon.
The moon sways women with their menses.
Men grow stronger and weaker
as it waxes and wanes.)

Now both the moon and the sun, shining from their sky paths, look after the People.
Moila, the Moon, watches by night, and Temet, the Sun, by day.

(No one can hide any wrongdoing
because they see it.)

4   The First People

Knowing death was in the world and determined to escape it,
>> some captains of the First People
>> gathered their friends and relatives
>>>>>> and flew to the sky.

Their hearts beat brightly as stars in the wide darkness.

The oldest and most important star captains,
>>>> surrounded by their relatives' fainter lights,
>> shine brightest.

Among them are:

>> Antares: Nükülish
>>>> and his right hand man
>> Arcturus: Nükülish po-ma
>>>> who rises first
>>>>>> to announce Antares's coming.

>>>> Antares's large group of followers
>>>>>> shine all around their old captain.

>> Altair: Yungavish (Buzzard)
>>>> and his right hand man
>> Vega: Yungavish po-ma

>>>> Altair's feather headdress sails just above him:
>>>> Pecheya Yungavish

>> Venus: Aylucha (Food Left Over From Evening Until Morning)
>>>> rises as the Evening and Morning Stars

>> The North Star: Tukmi iswut (The Heart of Wolves)
>>>> rises with his heart held in his three-fingered hand.

>>>> Residing in this still center,
>>>> his followers circle around him.

(Like stars circling the North Star,
people dance and march around the fire
during ceremonies in the sacred enclosure.)

The Three Stars of Orion's Belt and the Pleiades
rose to the sky about this time.

When the First People moved to the sky,
the Pleiades were seven sisters.
Just as the Star People let down a rope
for them to climb to the heavens,
Old Man Coyote came along.

Right away he noticed
they didn't have a man with them.
So he offered to help:
"You girls. I see you don't have a man going with you. I'll be your man."

The girls didn't answer but kept on climbing.
Noticing this, as fast as he could Coyote
hauled himself up the rope after them.

When the last sister reached safety, together they quickly cut the rope.

Coyote fell backwards through the sky,
becoming
the star Aldebran.

(This is why Aldebran always follows the Pleiades.
It's Coyote.)

Towish, the Milky Way,
the spirit's home,
streams across all of it.

(The cycling of stars, sun, and moon
shape the calendar of days,
months, seasons, and ceremonies,
the coming of crops,
                    migration of animals,
                    nesting of birds,
                              especially eagle.)

Old men, powerful doctors, carefully study
              the horizon
                    and the heavens
measuring the movement of the Sky People
              against shapes on the
              eastern horizon
                    and with wooden markers,
              arguing about the rising times
              of the stars, sun, and moon.

In the Simi Hills, at the shrine
              on top of Castle Peak
              at the mouth of Bell Canyon
              behind the village of Huwam
doctors gaze
              across the San Fernando Valley
              through a window in the rock
              to study the stars, sun, and moon
              rising on the eastern horizon.
The people
              around Ventura and Calabasas
call this shrine Tswaya tsuqele:
              The Feather Banner is Waving.

Some people call this mountain
              and the cave in its southwestern
              ridge, which is the home of the
              shaman Munits,
Kas'élewun:
                    Place of the Tongue.

Anywhere power
       moves through the Above and Below

19

Castle Peak: West Hills.

into the Middle World
and speaks to those
who have the knowledge-power
to understand
is Kas'élewun

After Wiyot died and the Star People settled in the sky,
Mountain Lion, Wolf, and Summer Thundercloud,
three great doctors,
knew the First People needed more ceremonies.

They drew the first ground painting. This painting is the universe.

(Ceremony leaders create ground paintings
in the sacred enclosure
when boys and girls are initiated
or when those who have been initiated die
and their feather headdresses are buried.)

For the girls' initiation painting, the three doctors dug a small pit

and called it: *tolmal* (navel)

the center of the Other World (Above and Below)
of the spirit after death.

Using earth removed from the center,
they formed a circle.

With colored sands and clays,
ground charcoal,
powdered plants and minerals,
they created the painting

The outer ring is white: The Milky Way
The middle ring is red: Tukmit, Dark Sky
The inner ring around the center is black:
The Spirit Root of Existence

They painted nine outward pointing diamonds around the center.
They painted many images inside the diamonds,
       and in the north they made a gate
               where the spirit escapes.

Inside the second diamond from the gate, there is a small circle: the ocean
           source of the breath of life,
               the air to breathe.

After the girls were instructed in the meaning of the painting,
      each spat a mouthful of salt and ground sage seeds
        into the center pit.

From its outer circle, they swept the painting into the pit
             —death-empyting—
               and tamped it down.

Other paintings,
    some in yellow, red,
      white, green, blue, black, red
mapped the world
with its flowers, grassy fields, and trees.

          (Sometimes doctors post four sticks
       or lengths of cane around the paintings
         in the north, east, south, and west.

         Cords of human hair or milkweed
       stretch from the painting to the posts,
           tying the spirit.

       When doctors shake the cords,
          the earth quakes.)

It was Eagle, Frog, Bear, Lion, Deer, and Raven
    who knew they needed more music
      for ceremonies and for pleasure.

Toovit, Brush Rabbit, had already used
the cocoon rattle at Wiyot's funeral
when he became
the First Singer.

So they decided to make the first flutes.

They made them by drilling four holes
in a hollowed elder branch
or in a stem of cane.

After practicing on their new flutes,
they decided to hold a contest to see
who could play the best tune
all in one breath.

Coyote heard about it and decided he'd like to give it a try.

Each player composed some tunes, and when all of them were ready,
they began to play for one another.

That's when Coyote showed up ready to go.

When it was his turn, he played his tune for very long time,
all in one breath.
It seemed like he was going to win.

Only Lizard didn't believe what he heard.
By watching Coyote carefully,
he discovered that at each small pause in the music,
Coyote drew a secret breath.

When it was Lizard's turn to play, he copied Coyote's scheme.
Coyote played again and then Lizard played again.

They played back and forth,
back and forth,
until Coyote,
tired and aggravated,
forgot to take his secret breath.

The clever Lizard won the contest,
and the People were freed from Coyote's trickery.

(Because the First People played musical
instruments when they sang and danced,
                    so do people today:

The four-holed flute made from
                    deer bone, cane, or elder

The shaman's rattle made from cocoons of the
                    Ceanothus moth

The deer hoof rattle

The turtle shell rattle filled with cherry,
                    manzanita, or palm seeds

The mountain goat bladder rattle

The gourd rattle

The deer bone whistle

Clapsticks used by striking together two
                    carved sticks

Split stick made by partly splitting
                    and binding the end
                    of a hollowed elder berry branch

Bull-roarer: a flat carved stick
                    tied with a double string;
                    when swung overhead,
                                        it roars
Singing stones: rare stones, when struck
                    against one another,
                                        ring like a bell.)

For the First People, music, singing, and dancing
                    create and send power,
                    shape the world, attract or repel,
                                        and give pleasure.

People from Ventura say that it was around this time,
after the death of Wiyot,
             that the gambling game began.

(Though other people say it may have begun long before that.)

Every night when Sun travels over the horizon and the world grows dark,
                    the Sky People aren't sleeping.

All night long they're sitting in the sky gambling house,
         singing their power songs,
                    playing the Bone Game.

Every night the stakes are the same:
                    the balance between
                    life and death.

The two teams kneel facing each other,
each lead by a captain and his teammate.

One team passes the deer bone dice—
             one white
             one marked black—
back and forth between the two of them
so no one can tell
             which of their four hands holds
                    the white bone
             and which one holds
                    the black marked bone.

The team holding the bones
sings its power songs
             to prevent the other team
             from seeing whose hand
                    holds which bone.

The other team sings
 to prevent them from having the power
             to hide the bones.
They sing to see right into their hands.

The words of my song spill from my heart.
I want you to answer them.

People, don't be silent!
People, answer my song!

The words of my song spill from my heart.
I want you to answer them.

The Ventura people say that Sun, captain of one team, is a cannibal.
As he travels across the sky, holding his fiery cottonwood bark torch,
he gathers people to eat.
He tucks the big ones into his belt
and the babies into his feather headband.

When he gets home at the end of the day,
he dumps them all on the floor
of his sky house
made of crystals
to share with his two daughters.
The daughters wear aprons
made of live rattlesnakes
with their tails looped at the top.

Their pets roam around the house:
tame bears, rattlesnakes,
elk, birds, wolves,
and mountain lions.

Evening Star, who is Eagle, is Sun's teammate.

Eagle, whose wings hold up the sky world,
lives alone in a far away house
made of white bones.

The captain of the other team is Sky Coyote:

the North Star
a creator who was there at the beginning.
Morning Star, who is rain and thunder, is his teammate.

Moon, who some people say is Datura, keeps score since she is neutral.

After singing for a long time
                    the team with the bones
                    stops moving them and holds out
                    closed hands.

The other team calls out what they see:
                    which hand holds the white bone
                    which hand holds the black marked bone.

If they call the bones right,
                    they get a point.

After enough points,
                    the bones change sides
                              and the game continues,
                    night
                              after night
                                        after night
                    until the Winter Solstice.

At the Winter Solstice,
                    the score is tallied.

                              (During the Winter Solstice,
                    Sun rests for five days in his house
                         at the most southern point
                                        in his yearly journey.

                    This is a dangerous time.
                    A time of ceremonies.)

If Sun wins,
          life goes out of balance.
                    Rains stop: heat, drought, destruction, death.

If Sky Coyote wins, the world stays in balance.
                    Rains come
                         as Sky Coyote
                                   pulls open the gambling house door
                                   showering the world with acorns,
                                   wild cherries, chia seeds,
                                        ducks, geese,
                                             all kinds of food.

Life is good and everyone eats well.

Then the game starts all over again.

(The outcome of the gambling game
—the outcome of everything—depends entirely
on the players' knowledge-power
and how well they use it.

This is why there is no accident,
no fortune,
no luck.

Doctors use their knowledge-power
to predict who will win the game.
They want to be certain the rains will come,
and that the world
will be renewed
and remain in balance.)

Around Tejon Ranch, a special doctor
an old man or woman,
speaks to Datura
while collecting her
and giving her to another doctor to drink
for visions revealing
who will win the gambling game.

During the Winter Solstice ceremonies,
around Ventura and Santa Barbara,
a Sun Doctor,
working to assure the rebirth
of the world
and to keep the sun and earth
balanced,

pulls the sun from his house

20

Toloache (*Datura wrightii*): also named Manit (Tongva) and
Momoy (Chumash) Marina del Rey.

urging him on his way north
using a Sun Stick:

Its wand is the axis of the world,
Its angled sandstone disc is the sun.

The disc, inlayed, painted,
and marked by degrees,
measures the progress of the sun.

People dance, sing, make offerings,
pay off debts,
and honor widows and orphan girls.

At the end of the solstice ceremonies,
they erect in certain sacred places
tall, painted, feathered, and beaded
Sun Poles.
For the rest of the year,
these shrines are kept clean and tended.

People visit them to leave offerings,
to sing about what they are feeling,
what they hope for
and what they need.

Certain shrines are only visited
by doctors with serious powers.

Between the shrine mountains, Pinos and Frazier,
in the Cuddy Valley,
the people of Ventura say,
lies the center of the world.

This is the most sacred of all places.

Spirits light fires there at night and dance,
play their flutes, whistles, and bull-roarers.
Dogs bark. The earth quakes.

In caves and rock shelters near the solstice ceremonies,

doctors paint or carve their visions on the walls,
                    images that activate
                              the power of what is painted.

In the Simi Hills
                    during the Winter Solstice ceremonies
                              at dawn doctors gather
                              to sing and hold rituals
                                        in a painted cave.

Focused by a notch in the sandstone cave's entrance,
                    a small triangle of light,
                                        like an arrowhead,
          pierces a target of five white circles.

The light shifts
                    into the shape of a finger
                    moving, left to right, over the mural's
                    pecked and polished wall
          with its red and white figures
                              painted on the blackened rock.

The light renews the life of the images
          and everything in the world they evoke.

The landscape is alive with shrines
          marked by painted, carved, or pitted rocks.

When Wiyot died and death entered the world,
          the people around San Juan Capistrano and San Luis Rey say
                    Tamaiyowit and Tukmit's son Takwish, Spirit Lightning,
                    took off from his house on Jamiwo, Mt. San Jacinito,
                              and began flying around the world.
His *ayelkwi* doesn't hold a shape, but flows into many forms.

Whenever Takwish leaves his mountain house
or returns in the evening,
the earth rumbles.

Jamiwo, Mt. San Jacinto, lives directly across
from his older brother, Piwipwi, Mt. San Gorgonio.
Both of these are First People.

(Shrines are often placed on mountains
because their power
is deep and strong.

People travel to mountain shrines
to leave offerings and to ask
for rain and food,
for protection against bears
and rattlesnakes,
and other necessities.)

No one can visit Takwish's house inside Lily Rock high up on the mountain.
A strong wind thick with dew blows so hard there
that it blinds anyone who comes near.

Occasionally Takwish stops over in Tahquitz Canyon near Palm Springs,
or at a rocky hill near Bernasconi Hot Springs,
or he rest in caves in the mountains just across the San Luis Rey River from Pala,
or he stays for awhile on the highest peak of Palomar Mountain.

(People far to the north, east, south, and west
have seen him flying in and out
of tall peaks in mountains ranges.)

Flying from his home to his favorite peaks and caves,
he looks like ball lightning,
or a whirlwind,
or he appears covered in feathers like a bird.
Sometimes down swirls off him like smoke and disappears
before it reaches the ground.

(No one wants to see Takwish.
He's a cannibal and spends the whole day gathering
handfuls of people to eat back at his cave.

He especially likes children and fat women.

During a great forest fire, sometimes Takwish hovers
over it, shining and whirling. If he's there,
it means someone is going to die in the fire.

When a person who is close to death
                    sees a great grandparent,
the dying person belongs to Takwish
                    who is hovering nearby
          trying to carry away another spirit.
When there is only a light floating away,
                              that means Takwish got it.)

                              Takwish is so powerful
          that even Tukuupar, Raven, whose name means Sky
                    and whose arrows are tipped with crystals,
          couldn't save his son from Takwish, who is his cousin.

          On one of his rounds looking for spirits to steal,
he grabbed Tukuupar's son
                    and ate him in his house on Mt. San Jacinto.
People searched three days for the boy but couldn't find him.

          Tukuupar is a doctor and can see into everything.
          That's how he saw his boy in Takwish's house.
          The next day Tukuupar set out to retrieve his son.
                              (Some people say that Tukuupar
                              was covered with hair
                              and came from Temecula.)

When he reached the house, an old woman—Takwish's mother—told Tukuupar
                    he'd better not stay or Takwish would eat him, too.
Just then Takwish returned with his load of people,
                    but right away he was suspicious.
                              He smelled something: it was Tukuupar.

21

Jamiwo (Mt. San Jacinto) rises 10,834 feet, the second highest peak in
Southern California: San Jacinto Mountains, Riverside County.

Takwish burst out laughing.
Thinking about eating his cousin made him very happy.
But Tukuupar was a great doctor and poisonous, too,
                                so he avoided every move Takwish made
            until Takwish settled down and decided to eat the dinner he'd brought home.

In his house, Takwish had everything people have:
                        an eating place, a fire,
                                    and plenty to eat and drink.
Tukuupar knew Takwish would invite him to share his food,
            so he had brought two rabbits to secretly roast
                        while Takwish roasted the people.
When it was time to eat, Takwish was so certain Tukuupar was eating the roasted people,
            he asked Tukuupar if he'd like something to drink
                        and pointed to a container of red fluid.
Nauseated by the thought of drinking human blood,
                                Tukuupar turned away in disgust and said no.
After dinner the two cousins stood around a fire outside the house.
Takwish, who was planning how he was going to capture Tukuupar,
                                        invited him to sing.
At first they argued, politely, about who should sing first.

Tukuupar won when he said, "I am someone from the outside and this is your house.
                        It is you who has the privilege of going first."
        "Okay, cousin, since you don't want to start, I will," said Takwish.

He began to dance while singing Tukuupar's secret power songs,
                                    trying to take control of him.
Tukuupar just laughed and made jokes, but he was thinking
                that he better stop Takwish before his singing started to work.
Tukuupar called little black biting flies
            to swarm around Takwish's face and ears
                    so he couldn't keep on singing or dancing.

Takwish, batting away the flies, cried out, "Cousin, look what you've done!
        You sent these flies! You're sending foul thoughts toward me."

When it was Tukuupar's turn to sing, he sang Takwish's power songs.

        Takwish started to worry.

    "Cousin," he asked, "how did you learn those songs?"

    "I sing with you every night, cousin. You just can't see me."

Takwish felt afraid.

"Cousin," Takwish said, "I also sing with you every night and day.
So, tell me, how did you come here?"

"In the same way that you travel to my house
                                    and no one sees you," said Tukuupar.

Tukuupar began to dance, leaping higher and higher,
                                    while Takwish sang Tukuupar's songs.
The mountain house was rocking and shaking so hard it was about to collapse.

"Enough!" cried Takwish. "Let's go back inside the house."

He felt very afraid.

When they were settled inside, Tukuupar said, "Cousin, I've come here to find out if my
son has fallen into your hands."
    "No," said Takwish, "I haven't seen him."

With that said, one by one, Tukuupar started untying and unrolling
                    Takwish's tall stack of ceremonial mats made of woven tule.
He knew Takwish used his power
            to cure the large and small scalps of the adults and children
            he had eaten—hair contains a person's spirit—
            and to roll each one in a mat that he tossed in a pile.
Takwish knew exactly where he had hidden the boy's scalp
                            —in an especially short and thick mat—
            but he was not going to give it to Tukuupar.
Each time Tukuupar's hand came close to it, he'd secretly move it aside.

    "No, that's not it. That one's not it either. You're not going to find it," Takwish
said. "If it were here, I'd give it to you first thing, cousin. What a mess you've made.
Now I have to tie up all those mats."

After he untied the last mat he could find, Tukuupar stood up and announced:
            "With my power to see, I am going find it."

He only had to leap into the air three times, singing:

            "I'm moving around, looking with second sight.
            I'm moving around, looking with ordinary sight.
            I'm trying the World Below.
            I'm trying the World Above"

when Takwish gave in.

"All right, all right. Don't break down my house. Here it is," he said, handing
over a mat.

Tukuupar unrolled it and carefully examined the scalp.
Turning it in his hands, he began to weep and started home.
As he walked away, Takwish mocked him: "Boo hoo, boo hoo, cousin."

Tukuupar turned around and said to Takwish,
"Oh, by the way, cousin, why don't you come to my house for our next
ceremony? A lot of fat people will be there, especially fat women. I'll let you know when you
should come."

When Tukuupar arrived home, he gathered the people and told them what had happened.
They all agreed to put on a ceremony in order to try Tukuupar's plan
to kill Takwish by jumping him when he arrived
and beating him to death with their strongest fire pokers.

When the date was set, Tukuupar personally invited Takwish.
It would be a big event with more people than usual attending.

As they planned, the people waited for Takwish, armed with fire pokers.
But, knowing better, Takwish didn't show up until everyone had gone to sleep.
He grabbed five or six of the fattest people and fled to his house.

There were so many people at the ceremony,
they never did figure how many he'd taken.
People kept asking who was missing.

The next evening Takwish returned to the ceremony,
but this time Tukuupar was waiting for him.
Politely, Tukuupar invited him to sit down.
When he did, the people rushed in and hit him as hard as they could.
They really pounded him.
At first it seemed like they couldn't kill him
because, over and over again, he kept getting up.
But finally he lay there
dead.
Exhausted, they dumped his body in the bushes.

For four days the people celebrated the death of the feared Takwish.

After the people had returned to their homes,
>five travelers came along
>>and found what looked to them like the body of a man
>>>rotting in the hot sun.

As they continued on their way, they said to one another:
>"That poor man. I wonder why they threw his body out there?"
Finally one of the men said,
>"Friends, we can't leave that body lying there. It needs to be cremated.
>That's what people do."

So they walked back,
>dragged the swollen and stinking body to a flat place,
>>piled some wood, put the body on top of it,
>>>and set it on fire.
The men stood around tending the pyre
>while the body of the shape-shifted Takwish burned
>>until only ashes, white bones, and a heart remained.

>Suddenly,
>>the heart exploded!

Fire scattered everywhere and the air was filled with thick black smoke.
The men jumped into a nearby spring to save themselves
>as flames consumed the entire arroyo, burning it clean.
From the water, the men saw a small piece of heart flopping around.
After the fire died down, they went over to examine it.
>>>A few minutes later,
>that scrap burst into the air
>>and flew away leaving a trail of smoke behind it.

>Takwish was alive!

The First People, the Ancient Ones:
>Bird People, Animal People, Tree People, everyone,
>continued talking in councils about how they should live,
>>how they should sing and dance,
>>>and who they should marry.

(Some people are homosexual.
Spirit guides select them when they are born.
The men wear the women's skirt
and do women's work.
They're prized as hard workers and
marry if they want to.)

The way they say it around Palm Springs,
every morning beautiful, intelligent
Moon Young Woman,
who cared deeply for her brothers and sisters,
invited them to join her at a pleasant sandy place where she
taught them how to make
cat's cradles using woven grass string.

She taught them how to run and laugh and wrestle,
how to run races,
and how to sing new songs.
She taught games for the girls
and games for the boys.

She instructed the women to rise early
and bathe at dawn before the men bathed.
She showed them how to shake out their long hair
to keep it from tangling
and to prevent the ends from blossoming.

Moon Young Woman instructed the First People
for a long time before the night when Mukat,
who the people around Palm Springs call the creator
and father of the First People,
found where she slept alone,
separate from the others.

Filled with lust, he cast a sleeping spell,
and then lay with her.

The next morning, sleepy and sore,
she called together her brothers and sisters
and sang a song about what had happened.
In her sorrow, she flew up to the sky, where she continued to
look after the People.

The First People were deeply sorrowful.
They missed their dear sister and teacher.

Mukat had turned mean.

He continued to play evil tricks on the People.

He gave Rattlesnake poisonous fangs
    by inserting into its mouth
        two of his gray whiskers
    so a single bite
      could kill.
He fooled the People into learning how
        to kill one another
    by pretending to teach them games,
and he ignored their grief
when they saw what they were doing.

This is how he brought death into the world.

Dismayed when they realized what was happening,
the First People decided
    to poison him by using his feces,
    though some people say it was his spit,
      to control his power.

Late at night, Lizard watched as Mukat,
        using his pipe smoke,
    cast a sleep spell over the People so they
    wouldn't know when he left the house
      to go defecate in the ocean.

The next day,
    Lizard reported to the People what he saw.

After Water Skipper failed to collect
    what they needed because
    the ocean waves drove him back,
Frog volunteered for the task.

From her hiding place below the water,
    Frog caught the feces,
calling it "This tobacco he eats and releases."

Mukat didn't hear it's usual thundering
                              as it hit the water.
At first he was suspicious,
                    and then he was afraid
              because immediately his body
                        grew swollen and weak.

Frog made sure half of the feces was scattered
                              by Water People.
She brought back the other half to be scattered
                              by Land People.

This way his power
              could never be put back together,
              assuring that Mukat could never be cured.

He was going to die, and he did,
              despite all the doctors he called to cure him.

The People burned his house and cremated Mukat,
              but the fire wasn't out
                        when Coyote leaped onto the pyre,
              stole his heart,
                        and ran away to eat it.

When many new plants grew out of the place
                        where Mukat's ashes were buried,
one of the People followed the creator's tracks
              a very long way
                        until he found Mukat's spirit.

After complaining that he would have told them
              about the plants
                        if they hadn't killed him,
Mukat gave careful instructions
              about how these plants,
              and all the plants they would eat,
                  were his body
                        as was the Big House
              where they would do ceremonies.

Despite what he had done,
the First People were deeply sorrowful
about the death of Mukat.
He was their father
and they were his children.
His power had created the world.

(This is why people sing after gathering plants
and bringing them to the Big House.

These are the body of Mukat.)

Before all this happened,
Moon Young Woman had divided the First People
into two groups.

She took one group far off to a special place
where she taught them how to sing their own songs
and perform their own ceremonial dances.
Then she took the other group
and taught them their special songs and dances.

She taught both groups
how to build the ceremonial Big House
and how to choose a ceremony leader.
This man, with the other leaders,
would guide the clan,
look after the ceremonial house,
learn all the songs and histories,
and keep the sacred bundle
called "Heart of the Big House."

She taught them ceremonies
for singing in song contests
against one another.

She taught them how to sing against their enemies
in Song Wars.

(Feuds between families and villages
are usually fought in
Song Wars:

eight days singing nasty, insulting songs
while stomping on the ground
as though on the grave of the enemy.

The power of the songs
harms the enemy.)

Finishing her instructions,
she told one group to leave the Big House
and then to return
singing and dancing their new songs.

When they concluded, the other group sang
while the opposite group danced.

She told them that they must do this from now on
because now one group belonged to
Coyote
the other belonged to
Wild Cat.

This is because, according to the people around Palm Springs,
the First World's creators are
older brother, Mukat, who is
Coyote
and younger brother, Temayawet, who is
Wild Cat.

They would organize themselves,
according to their ancestor,
and always marry someone
from the other lineage.

The ground for my new house is leveled,

It is leveled for my house of green willow boughs.

To the new couple are given five gifts:
This sweet, roasted core of the yucca
This soapstone cooking pot
This ritual sand
This dark, sweet honey from the burrowing bee
This toasted white sage seed.

The First People:
reasonable, willful, emotional, powerful,
lived well in the First World
keeping the balance for a very long time.

One day, the ocean began to rise.

Great breakers crashed over the beaches
                                    and rushed across the plains.
Seawater filled the valleys and covered the mountains.

                        Soon water covered the whole world.

Some of the First People escaped
            by climbing to the top of a nearby hill, Katukto.

                        This hill is one of the First People.

Katukto slowly rose higher and higher
            as the People watched the ocean
                        cover even the tallest peaks.

Those who fled to Katukto survived.

                        (On top of Katukto
                        still lie the heaps of shells
                        left over from the shellfish eaten
                        by the First People while they waited
                        for the ocean to recede.

                        Ash and stones
                        reddened from their cooking fires
                        are still there, too.)

        The way people in Ventura say it,
                        rain started and wouldn't stop
                                    as the ocean waters rose.

Only Spotted Woodpecker survived because he flew
        to the top of the tallest tree in the world.

When the water reached his feet,
        he cried out to his uncle, Sun:
  "I'm drowning, Uncle. Pity me! Help me!"

The Sun's two daughters heard him.
They saw how stiff and cold he was
      and begged their father to help him.

Sun agreed and held his blazing torch so close to the water
      that it steamed and started to recede.

Warmed by the Sun, Spotted Woodpecker was able
    to snatch from the water
    the two acorns Sun tossed to him.
Sun tossed two more acorns close to the tree.
Woodpecker ate those and was no longer hungry.

(That's why woodpeckers love to eat acorns.)

When the flood was over, Spotted Woodpecker was alone.

    (Rocks in the mountains still hold the shape
      of the First People who drowned.
  They were very tall and could wade
      across to the islands with their carrying nets
      full of chia and acorns
      to trade with the Islanders.
  Very old people have seen their huge bones,
      yards long, on Santa Rosa island.)

After the water receded and the ground dried,
    the First People left Katukto and climbed
  to the top of Kalaupa, Santiago Peak:
    "Place of the Timber"

        (the tallest peak in the Santa Ana Mountains
        and tallest of the pair called Saddleback).

Here they sacrificed a bear and sat together in a council.
They talked about whether or not they should go any farther.
                                        They weren't certain what they should do.

A big crowd of First People decided to travel to Lake Elsinore.

When they arrived, Blackswift and Kingbird had their first menses.
The People held a ceremony for them.
When it was over, Blackswift and Kingbird felt so good
            they composed some songs.
                                (Their songs are still sung
                                at the conclusion of the girls' initiation.)

From Lake Elsinore, the First People dispersed
                        north, east, south, west,
                                    in all directions.

            The First World was coming to an end.
            Everything was changing.

5 *Human Beings:*
Singers, Balance Keepers

22

Valley oak (*Quercus lobata*) is a source of
edible acorns: Santa Monica Mountains.

As the First People traveled in all directions, some petrified
leaving huge bones
or footprints in stone
to mark the track of their migration.
Others became stars
Others became the winds
Others became the landscape: hills, mountains,
springs, rivers, trees,
rocks, animals, and plants.

All of these are the bodies of the First People
the Ancient Ones
the Ancestors.

The migrating groups of First People painted rocks
and made many other marks as they traveled
to show where they rested and what they claimed.
These marked places, stones, and trees
are the bodies of a family's Ancestors
and record their lineage.

In some places, they scooped out a rock
to mark their claim to that spot.
Or they marked and carried along a rock
to leave at a place they claimed,
like the Turtle Rock near Temecula.
This is a family's Ancestor.

In some places they made a rock very smooth by sliding on it.
This rock is a family's Ancestor.

In some places, their bodies shifted into stone.
One of these is a painted boulder in the shaped of a woman.
Small sacred stones lie balanced on top of her body.

          (A wave of the hand could move them,
               but they remain where they are.
          People in pain rub against the boulder
              for relief and healing.)

On a hill named "Sacred Feather Headdress,"
an oak tree grows through the rocks.
             This tree is a family's Ancestor.

Along the way, if a group needed water,
          they sang a water song.
When the water appeared, they claimed that place as part of their story.

          As they migrated to their new homes,
the First People sang about their experiences:
     where they stopped along their journey,
      what they discovered,
        the marks they made as they traveled,
        and where they settled.

          (Each family has songs about its Ancestors
            and where they settled.
          These songs are the deed
            to the family's homeland.

          Each family has its songs about the creation
            and lives of the Ancestors.
          These songs show how people are related.

          All songs are hereditary.
          No one sings another family's songs.

          If a lineage dies out, songs can be given
          as a gift to someone in another family.

          Songs can heal.
          Songs can kill.

Individuals have their songs,
Ceremonies have their songs,
known by everyone who takes part.
Doctors have their ceremonial songs
and they have their secret songs.)

The First People,
everything we see: stars, stones, wind, and waters,
the furred, finned, and feathered,
bushes and trees,
are the Ancestors of the new people,
the human beings.

Just as the First People migrated throughout the world, the new people,
the human beings, traveled, too,
seeking their homelands.
Wherever they settled, they told stories and sang songs
about their Ancestors and where they came from.

Along the coast, around San Juan Capistrano and north,
they say human beings were made this way:

After Wiyot's ashes and bones were ground and buried,
the First People gathered in a council at Povungna,
the village in Long Beach where some say Wiyot died.

They were talking about how to solve the problem of gathering food and eating it.
White clay no longer nourished them and they were tired of it.

While they talked, some human beings wandered in,
sat down at the council
and asked what they were discussing.
Children of Tamaiyowit, the humans had been wandering the earth for a very long time
until they made their way to Povunga
and found the First People.

They told the council that they had the power to create food.

The human beings gave new powers to the First People.
          Some would cause rain and weather.
               Some would cause grains, greens, and roots to grow.
                 Others would cause the animals to flourish.

They would do these things by singing new songs
               taught to them by the human beings.

As they sang their powerful songs, the First People turned into the new world,
               transformed into whatever they dreamed of eating.

This is the world where the human beings live and what they eat.

Among all the people, the human beings are the ones who have the power,
        through their songs,
            to affect the balance of the world.

Around Palm Springs, people say human beings
        were formed by the twin creators:
           older brother, Mukat,
              and younger brother, Temayawet.

In the beginning: darkness.
One was female.
One was male.

In the darkness,
        red, white, blue, brown
        twisted to a point
        whirled to a ball, a substance:
           two embryos wrapped in a placenta.
But they were stillborn.

Once again the lights whirled.
Two embryos became children,
        brothers who asked one another:
          "Who are we?"

They stretched and rolled
                until they made a hole
            where they emerged and named themselves:
            Mukat and Temayawet

In the darkness they argued.

Since what comes first is always most powerful,
           these two were always arguing
                    about who was eldest
           and therefore most powerful.

           After their first argument,
the twins emerged slowly into darkness,
           pulled pipes and tobacco from their hearts,
           and sat together smoking.
Mukat drew black tobacco.
Temayawet drew white tobacco.

Temayawet asked: "How can we light our tobacco?"
Mukat answered:
        "You say you are older than I am,
           yet you don't know how to light our pipe!"
Mukat drew the sun from his mouth,
                  but it was too fast.
It slipped away into the darkness.

Mukat drew from his heart the West Light.
Temayawet drew from his heart the East Light.
Mukat lighted his pipe with these,
                blowing smoke into clouds.
He held up his pipe
           but told Temayawet he was holding it down.
Temayawet looked below to find it.

Then Temayawet held up his pipe
             but said he was holding it down.
Mukat knew where it was and took it.

This proved he was eldest.

After they smoked,
Mukat said they would draw from their hearts

        the center pole of the world,
          which they called
             Heart of the World.
But it would not stand.
They drew snakes from their hearts
    and told them to secure it,
        but it moved.
They told two rocks to hold it,
        but it moved.
They drew spiders from their hearts,
    and their webs woven in the four directions
        held it still.

Singing and calling themselves by name,
    Mukat and Temayawet climbed the center pole.
Looking down from their seats
    at the top of the center pole of the world,
      they saw,
          rising from their afterbirths,
          swelling clouds of smoke
           that carried disease and sickness.
Mukat said there would be men and women
    who would have the power
        to cure disease.
He called these people-to-come: doctors.

Next they decided to create
      the four directions
        and then the earth.

Mukat drew black earth from his heart.
Temayawet drew white earth from his heart.

On their second try, they secured the earth
      on top of the center pole of the world
    by calling from their hearts black and white spiders
      to spin webs to hold it in place.

They sent ants and two whirlwinds
      to spread earth in all directions.
Because it shook so much,
    they bordered the earth with ocean
    and two water demons to hold it in place.

They filled the ocean with seaweed for the sacred mats,
other sacred creations, and all kinds of water creatures.

They drew the sky from their hearts
                    and secured it with two whirlwinds
                    at the edges of the earth
          and blew their saliva into the sky to create stars.

Looking around, Mukat and Temayawet decided
                    that the earth needed creatures to live on it.

The brothers' mother and father, the Two Nights,
          circled around, humming,
                    singing lullabies to soothe their twin sons
                    while they created the first human beings.

(This is why, calmed by their songs, people sleep at night.)

While smoking tobacco, they created dog,
          but the smoke harmed his eyes,
          so he was never again able to see
                    as well in the day as in the night.

Then they drew from their hearts Coyote,
                    who assisted with the creation,
          and Owl who helped by seeing in the dark.

          Working slowly, carefully,
Mukat took the black earth
          and shaped the first human beings
                    with the bodies they have today.

Temayawet worked carelessly, quickly.
          His people had faces on both sides of their heads.
                    They had fingers and toes like a dog's paws.
                    They had four legs and bellies on both sides.

As each human being was finished,
          Owl hooted and Coyote carried it
                    to each brother's separate pile.

When all was completed, the brothers argued about whose creation was best:

Was it better to be able to see in both directions at once?
Would things fall through hands with separate fingers
                    instead of paws?
Was it better for the body to be shaped like a dog?
Or was it better to have a back and shoulders for carrying things
                        and arms for drawing back an arrow in the bow?

Temayawet argued that they wouldn't need bows and arrows
                        because there wouldn't be any shooting.

Mukat said pretty soon there would be.

            Temayawet said there would be no death.

Mukat said there would be death.

            Temayawet said that if his people got old, he would dip them
                        in water and make them young again.
                        If they died,
                        he would bring them back to life.

Mukat said if he brought them back, they would stink like rotten meat.

            Temayawet said he would clean his people with clay
                        and smoke them with grass and willow
                        until they smelled sweet.

Mukat argued that if he did this, the world would soon be too small
        because of the new people being born.

            Temayawet said he would simply stretch the world wider.

Mukat said, in that case, soon the people would run out of food.

            Temayawet said the people could eat the earth.

Mukat said that soon the earth would be gone, completely eaten.

When the argument was over, Mukat, the elder brother, had won again.

Enraged, Temayawet used his breath to open
                        a great crack in the earth near Indian Wells.

He plunged all the way to the center of the earth
                              while trying to take everything with him.

Mukat warned his brother to take only what he had created.
                Everything else had to stay where it was.

Originally the earth was smooth and flat,
                but as Mukat struggled with his brother
                              to prevent him from taking all they had created,
                              the world shook and buckled.
Violent winds blew and the sky warped and waved.

Fixing the ground with his knees,
                Mukat used one hand to hang on to his creatures
                              and the other to hold up the sky.

Temayawet managed to take with him only those he had created
                except the moon, the palm, the coyote, and the wood duck
                              who were left behind.
Some people say that the fly and the hero Eagle Flower also were left behind.

When the fighting ended and calm returned to the earth,
                              the land was no longer flat and smooth.
Mountains and canyons remained,
                the ground was rough,
                              and water filled the new streambeds.

                In the darkness, Mukat's children,
                    our ancestors,
                    the first human beings,
                    came to life.

At that time, when the new sun first rose in the east
                and the new people could see one another,
                              dog was still able to talk with them.
But as the sun rose higher, he lost this ability,
                though in his heart dog still knows everything.

Around Ventura and Santa Barbara,
people say that human beings
were created this way:

After the great flood
when everyone on earth was destroyed,
except Spotted Woodpecker,

Sun,
Sky Coyote (who is the star Polaris),
Moon (Old Woman Momoy who is Datura),
Morning Star (who is rain and thunder),
Eagle (who is Evening Star)
all gathered in a council to discuss
how they would create human beings.

Sky Coyote announced that he wanted
new people in the world
and that he wanted them to look like him
since he had the best hands.
Eagle disagreed about the hands.

Lizard attended the council
but kept quiet
and just listened to the arguments.

Finally, Sky Coyote convinced the council
that his was the best plan.

The next day they all gathered in the sky
at a perfectly round, flat-topped boulder
made of such a fine white stone
that it kept the impression of whatever touched it.

At the ceremony, Lizard positioned himself
right behind Sky Coyote.

Just as Sky Coyote reached out his paw
to stamp its impression in the stone,
Lizard shot out one of his hands
and stamped his print into the rock.

Sky Coyote was furious and chased after Lizard,
trying to kill him.

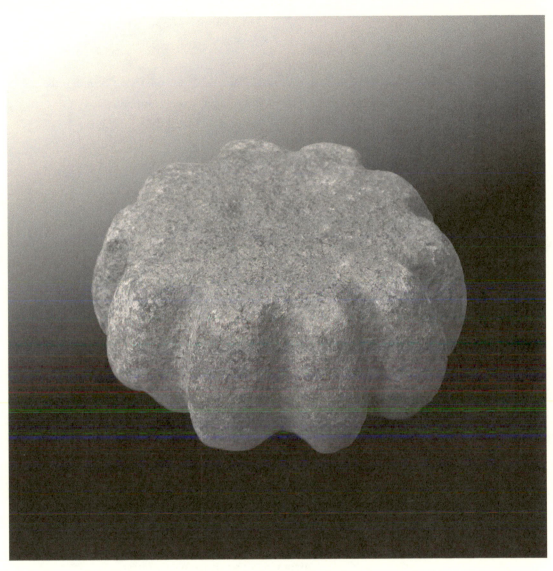

23

Cogged stone. This small, perfectly round and symmetrical carved granitic
stone was recovered in 1927 with twelve others in what was probably a
ceremonial cache on the Rancho Cienega ó Paseo de la Tijera. Perhaps
used in sun rituals or as a symbol of stars, thus far these stones are found
only in areas known to have been occupied by the Tongva: Baldwin Hills.
Courtesy of the Southwest Museum of the American Indian, Autry
National Center of the American West, Los Angeles; 203.L.6A.

But Lizard darted into a crevice and escaped.

There was nothing Sky Coyote could do
                                    to change what had happened
                    since Sun and Eagle were happy about it.

                    (This is why people today have hands
                    like Lizard's and not paws.
                    That rock is still there in the sky
                                        with Lizard's print.)

The next topic for discussion by the council
                    was whether or not the new people should die.
Sky Coyote argued against death,
                    saying that when they got old,
                    he would throw them into a lake to make them young again.

But the council disagreed saying,
                    if he did that, the world would soon be so full of people
                    there wouldn't even be standing room.

Sky Coyote lost this one, too, and so the new people would have to die.

                    When they die, their spirits hover here for three days,
                        before traveling west with the sun
                                over Point Conception to the Other World,
                                    following the trail of the Milky Way.

On its journey, each spirit passes through
                    the Land of the Widows
                    who come out in tears to greet it.
                                The Widows, always youthful,
                    revive themselves
                                by bathing in a shallow spring
                    and eat by breathing their food.

Flying through a narrow and deep ravine,
                    the spirit must dodge clashing rocks that kill anyone
                    living who tries to pass into the next world.

24

Raven (*Corvus corax*).

Two Ravens swoop down to peck out the spirit's eyes.
The spirit, finding poppies in the ravine,
      fixes one into each empty socket
            and can see again.

Along the way the spirit flies past the huge
      scorpion-woman
            who threatens to sting if it
                flies too close.

Beyond this are the waters that separate
      the world of the living
               from the world of the dead.

Evil spirits, who have faces
      but whose bodies are stone, line the shore.

A gigantic tree trunk, cut and stripped
        into a pole that ceaselessly rises and falls,
                bridges the two worlds.

As the spirit carefully starts across the pole,
        two terrifying monsters
                rise out of the water.
If a spirit's knowledge-power is weak, if it is ignorant,
if it has no spirit helpers, if it never drank *toloache*,
        it falls into the water
      and is transformed into a frog, a toad,
                a salamander, or a fish.
If a spirit's knowledge-power is strong,
        it crosses safely to the Other World,
            a land of happiness and plenty.

After twelve years enjoying the Other World,
        the spirit is reborn in this world.

It's all a circle.

Some old people call it "an eddy within an abyss."

Other people say that once a spirit
      arrives in the Other World,
        it never grows old
          and it never leaves.
The Other World is packed full of spirits.

The new people, the human beings,
      think of Sky Coyote as their father
      and turn to him when they need help.
From his home in the sky,
      he always looks after his children

(The other Coyote, the trouble–maker,
      is the star Aldebaran.)

Like the First People,
    the human beings seeking their new homelands,
           claimed the places named in their songs,
      though this could lead to disputes.

Sometimes the human beings left one homeland for another
            because conditions changed
      and they were out of balance with the land.

That's how people came to live around San Juan Capistrano.

Oyaison was captain of a large village, Sejat,
   in the San Gabriel Valley
   named after the burrowing bee.
 His wife, Sirorum, was named
   for the shaking and clacking of the shells,
         beads, and deer hoof rattles
         attached to her skirt and jewelry.

They had three children, and the oldest
   was their only daughter, Coronne,
       which means Red Ladybug
   and designates a woman who is the captain.

Oyaison's rapidly growing village
   was quickly using up the seeds and animals
       which were their food.
So, after Sirorum died, Oyaison decided
   to divide his people, and with one group,
      he and Coronne moved south.

They settled by a spring
   in the San Juan Capistrano Valley
     near Trabuco Creek.

When the village was established,
Oyaison named Coronne its captain
    and returned north to his village.
The people held a celebration
   that lasted several days
      to honor Coronne.
They danced, sang, played games, and feasted
   with guests from many neighboring villages.

Coronne was huge and her navel stood out,
    so the people named their new village Putuidem: "The Navel."

Her village soon became large, prosperous,
    and the center of ceremonial life
        for people in the smaller villages founded nearby.

      One night during the celebration,
          while she was sleeping,
      Coronne's body swelled until it burst
        and became a mound of earth.
      The people of Putuidem deeply mourned her death.

      The next night, people who were leaving
        the celebration for their home villages,
          men women and children,
            slept nearby in a great pile.

      People say that when they woke up,
        they called themselves the Acjachemen:
          mound of living beings.

      Now they would be a new people, different from
        the people of the San Gabriel Valley,
        with a new language and new ways.

Like the First People,
    the human being's knowledge-power
        was strongest right after their creation.
Because power is always greatest at the beginning
      and weakens over time,
    everything at the beginning is more potent
        than what comes after.

      The human beings' work is to keep the world in balance
   and to perform ceremonies to renew its vitality
      and slow its decline.

Knowledge, caution, good sense,
                self-restraint and moderation, taking counsel,
            honesty, dependability, and practicality,
                honoring the ceremonial exchanges between villages,
                hospitality,
all these keep the world in balance
                and lead to wisdom.

Imbalances, like selfishness, cause serious trouble, even war.

(Doctors use their knowledge-power
                to heal and protect their people
                    from all forms of harm and imbalance
                    by controlling invisible forces
                        including the powers of strangers.
With their skills, they defend their villages
                    during wars or feuds with their neighbors.

Doctors know how power trades shapes,
                    how it flows between people
                        with similar potency,
            like human being, grizzly bear, and hawk.

With the help of datura, crystals and other power objects,
                        and their spirit guides,
                doctors send themselves into other forms
                    or far away
                —to cause rain, to heal, to gain new powers,
                        sometimes even to kill—
            whatever they wish.

Some of their songs, like maps,
                define boundaries and territories.

Sometimes doctors compete
                to see who has the most power.

Doctors with great skills might be feared
                and live separately from their villages.)

Rawi'jawi was a very powerful doctor

and captain of the village of Tujunga.

He had two children, a boy and a girl.

His daughter, who had beautiful, thick, glossy black hair so long it touched her feet,

married the captain of the village to the east (near Glendale)

and went to live there.

She didn't return home to visit her parents

until after the birth of their first child, a son.

When the boy was old enough to travel, the captain asked his wife

to take their son to meet his grandparents.

"Yes, why not," she said.

So he sent out a few boys to kill a deer for her to present as a gift to her parents.

When she was ready to leave, he assigned a girl to travel with her to carry the deer.

"No, that's not necessary," she said.

With the deer over her shoulder and the baby in her arms,

she set out for her parent's home in Tujunga.

When the sun was high and the weather was very hot,

she stopped to rest by a pool

beside a rock pitted with a group of small mortars.

Feeling refreshed, she collected wood,

built a fire,

roasted the deer,

and ate the whole thing except for the bones.

The next morning she pounded the bones into meal and ate them all.

She drank some water, picked up her son, and walked back to her home.

When she arrived, her husband, the captain, questioned her:

"Where have you been?

Why have you returned so soon?

How are your parents? What did they give you to eat?"

"I came back because they had nothing for us to eat,

only water mixed with dried and ground cactus fruit," she answered.

Fifteen days later, the captain, her husband, said to her,
> "Don't you want to take some food to your parents since they are so poor?"
> "Yes," she answered, "why not."

He didn't assign a girl to travel with her this time,
> but watched her walk off alone
>> carrying a deer over her shoulder with their son in her arms.

She stopped at the same place she had stopped before, roasted the deer,
>> and ate the whole thing except for the bones.
In the morning, she pounded the bones into meal, ate them all, drank some water,
>> and returned.

When she arrived, her husband questioned her:
> "Where have you been?
>> Why have you returned so soon?
>>> How are your parents? What did they give you to eat?"

> "I came back because they had nothing for us to eat,
>> only water mixed with dried and ground cactus fruit," she answered.

Not knowing what to do, the captain, her husband, called his people to a council
> where they discussed the situation.
They suspected that his wife was not telling the truth.
> For one thing, living on ground cactus fruit was impossible.
In fifteen days, they advised, he should kill another deer,
> give it to his wife to take to her parents,
>> and assign a girl to travel with her.
This girl would be warned that she would be killed
> if she didn't tell the truth about what happened.

In fifteen days, the captain gave his wife a deer
> and forced her to take the girl with her
>> on her journey to visit her parents.

When they came to the pool where she had stopped before,
> the wife said to the girl,

"I always stop here.

      I don't go all the way to my parents' house because it's too far away.

        Let's rest."

After awhile she ordered the girl to gather firewood for roasting the deer.

Together they ate the whole thing and in the morning pounded and ate all the bones.

      "Let's drink some water and go back," said the wife.

      "You will help me lie. Don't tell anyone we ate the deer."

The girl agreed and they walked back to their village.

When they arrived, the captain asked his wife the usual questions,

      and she answered as she had before.

That night the captain and his council took the girl to the council house

        and threatened to kill her

          if she didn't tell the truth about what happened.

The girl agreed to tell the whole story:

      The wife said she didn't go all the way to her parents because it was too far.

      She always stopped at the same place where she cooked and ate the deer.

      In the morning she pounded and ate the bones, drank some water,

        and ordered her not to say anything to the captain, her husband.

      "Now you can see for yourself," said the councilors. "That woman's a phony!"

      "How can I punish her?" asked the captain.

      "She's a big water drinker. She drinks water every night.

          Order everyone to empty their water jars or hide them.

          In the last house leave one jar filled with urine.

          On the night when you do this,

        you must sleep in a corner of the council house with your wife,

        and all the men of the village will sleep there, too,

             naked and face up."

That night the wife woke up as usual feeling terribly thirsty.

             She needed to find a water jar.

Since it was very dark, with her hands in front of her and her fingers spread out,

        she carefully felt her way to the door.

      "Ahh!" she cried, "Oh!" as she accidentally touched the men's penises.

The men said nothing.

At last she got out the door and searched from house to house for some water,
                                              but all the containers were dry.
When she reached the last house, the people who lived there asked her,
        "What are you doing?"
        "I'm dying of thirst," she said, "and nobody has any water."
Pretending innocence, they said, "Who knows what's in this jar. Go ahead and look."
She took the jar of urine, drank it all without noticing what it was,
                                        and returned to the dark council house.

Slowly she felt her way back to where she was sleeping in the same way she had left,
        crying out as she accidentally touched the men.

When she woke up very early in the morning and lifted her head,
        she found that all her hair had all fallen out
            and lay by her head in a heap.
                            Her head was as bald as her hand.
Quickly she rolled the hair into a ball,
        put it under her left armpit, picked up her baby,
            and left the dark council house very carefully
                        because she wasn't coming back.
She felt her way out, touching the men just as she had before, and walked away.

The wife traveled for a long time until and she was exhausted
                            and the baby started crying with hunger.

Angrily she said to her son, "It's all because of you that they insulted me."

She took him by the ankles and dashed his head against a rock.

        (You can still see the red stain of his blood on that boulder.)

When she arrived at her parents' home in Tujunga
                she crawled into a large granary basket
                    stored in the cave where they kept their food.
In the morning, her old mother opened the basket to get some seeds
                and discovered her daughter, bald-headed, hiding there.
Frightened, she cried out, "You scared me! Why are you here? Why have you come?"

When she told her mother what had happened,
        the old woman asked her daughter
                if she had any idea how to make her hair grow back.
Finally she said, "All right, you had better stay hidden."

Because it was the rule that everyone bathes each morning before dawn to stay healthy,
      her mother told her that she would have to bathe in her brother's spring.
          But she must stay alert because if he discovered her there,
                    he might kill her.
No one ever bathed in her brother's spring. He was the captain's son.

The first morning after she bathed in her brother's spring,
              he was surprised to find the water riled.
It wasn't exactly dirty but it wasn't clean either,
              so he knew someone else had bathed there.
He decided to arrive early the next morning to see if he could see
                who was bathing in his pool.
But when he arrived, again the water was disturbed.
By now he hadn't bathed for two days and this left him feeling weak.

"This time I'm really going to grab you," he said.
"Tomorrow I'll be here even earlier. I have to find out who is doing this."

When he arrived, it was still dark, so he couldn't see that it was his sister
             who was seated in the water
"I got you," he shouted as he dragged her out,
        kicked her away from the water,
          and walked home angry.

Crying, the girl fled to the cave where she gathered up her hair,
           the basket where she had hidden, a carrying net,
              and marched away.
She arrived at a spring where women fill their water jars.
Seated at the edge of the water was a baby
             who looked just like her baby.
    "Oh, how did you get here!" she cried as she picked it up
              and held it close to nurse.
That baby
     sucked and sucked and sucked
          until it swallowed her completely.

People know what happened because they found the hair, the basket, and the net.
It wasn't her baby. It was the underwater monster who takes any form.

Some people call it Mother of the Water.

The girl's mother was filled with grief.
When Rawi'jawi found her crying, she told him the whole story,

(except she didn't know that in the early morning darkness
their son couldn't see who was in his pool,
nor could he tell whether it was a man or a woman).

She was very angry at their son, the young captain, and so was Rawi'jawi.

Without taking counsel, he decided to avenge his daughter.

The people of Tujunga loved the young captain and they treated him like a son.
Rawi'jawi knew they would never kill him.

Instead, he paid Munits to do it.

Munits was a cannibal who lived in a large cave on the back side of Castle Peak
called by some people Kas'élewun, Place of the Tongue,
because of its power to talk to doctors.

One day the people of Tujunga were gathered around the boy
while the young people played games, danced, ran races,
and otherwise enjoyed themselves.
The elders sat in a circle around the young captain,
talking with him and enjoying the young people.

From the direction of Castle Peak they saw an old man walking toward them.

Some people cried out, "Don't let him touch our young captain!"
Others said, "Oh, what harm can such an old man do?"

When the old man arrived, he said,
"Won't you let me greet your young captain? I have a gift for him."
He held an owl, the kind that lives in caves.

The people talked it over,

        and since more said yes, to let him give the gift, than said no,

    they let the old man hand the owl to the boy.

But the owl, who was a doctor, too, flapped out of the boy's hands

        and flew around tempting the people to catch him

While everyone was running after the owl,

    the old man grabbed the boy, gripped him in his armpit,

      and walked away laughing.

The elders were the first ones to see what had happened.

The young people were still shouting and running around after the owl

        which they never caught.

The young captain had twenty young men who were as his companions and bodyguards.

    Each one was twenty years old, a fast runner, and a good fighter.

At last they heard what the old men were saying and ran after Munits,

      who carried the young captain to his cave.

    They couldn't catch him. He was swift as a bird.

The bodyguards and all the people of the village

    gathered at the foot of the cliff beneath the cave

      and shouted at Munits to give them their young captain.

"Sure, here's your captain," cried Munits, as he threw an arm bone

out one of the slits in the cave. Through another slit he tossed the other arm bone.

    One by one, he threw the bones of each part of the young captain's body

      through different slits until, finally,

        he tossed them the boy's head.

The people gathered the bones and, crying, took them to Rawi'jawi

    who was filled with grief and regret.

He decided to kill Munits.

    "You're going to pay!" he shouted. "I'm going to have you killed."

To do the job, Rawi'jawi hired a flying doctor who usually appeared as a sparrow hawk.

    "I've killed my own son," he told Sparrow Hawk, who only said, "All right."

Munits liked to rest just beyond his cave on Castle Peak,

    a place where people observe the passage of the stars, sun, and moon.

25

Exterior of the Cave of Munits: West Hills.

He had eaten a massive amount of yellow clover
> and fell asleep face up with his swollen belly shining like the sun.

When Sparrow Hawk found Munits, he began diving at him.
But Munits had seen him coming and decided to grab some of his feathers,
> since, like all the doctors, he wore hawk feathers in his nose hole.
"Come on, attack me," taunted Munits.

In an instant when Munits was careless, Sparrow Hawk swooped in,
> ripped open his stomach, spilling his guts
>> and killing the evil doctor. It was a stinking mess.

> (This is why yellow clover is bitter.
> Before this happened, all clover was sweet.)

When Rawi'jawi returned to his wife, he found that she was gone.
> In her grief at losing both her daughter and her son,
>> she had walked into the mountains behind Tujunga
>> and turned into stone.
>> (She is still seated there.)

Rawi'jawi was overcome with grief. He had lost his entire family.
> He covered his face and hands with ashes he never washed off
> and wandered into the mountains to die.

After he crossed the mountains, he came to a village
> where several women were harvesting cactus fruit.
> They put the fruit into a net held at each end,
>> and a third woman hit it with a stick.
The wind carried off the spines.

> "What are you doing? How are you?" Rawi'jawi asked them.

> "We are well. How are you? And where are you going?" the women replied.

> "I'm seeking my death," said Rawi'jawi. "I've come here among you so you will
stab me in the eyes with those spines to blind me and help me die."

Rawi'jawi sat down, against the wind, with his chin sticking out and his eyes wide open.

Some of the women nudged the others and said, "Come on, let's stick them in his eyes."
Some said no, they didn't want to.
But there are always people who are meaner than others, and they prevailed.

The women shook and hit the net, but the spines flew into their own eyes,
blinding every one of them.
They died right there of hunger, thirst, and exposure
because no one was able to lead them home.

"Ha!" said Rawi'jawi. "You mocked me when I was suffering.
Now you know what it feels like to suffer."

He walked away from the blind women, crossed another mountain,
traveled north and northeast, south and southwest,
visited the coast, and started back to Tujunga.

Once again he crossed over a mountain and came to a very large village.
This time the women were in a room underground making baskets.

Once again he asked them to help him die
by blinding him with the awls they were using to make their baskets.
Once again some people wanted to do it, and others did not.
The mean ones won, and as they stabbed Rawi'jawi in the eyes,
their own eyes burst out of their heads and they were all blinded.

"You mocked me when I was suffering," said Rawi'jawi as he walked away.
"Now you see suffering."

He climbed another mountain and from the top
he could see a large village holding ceremonies.

"I'm going to enter the village, so they will seize me and attempt to kill me.
I'm going to go!" he cried as he turned into an eagle and swooped down to the village.

Of course, he was going to kill them instead.
There was nothing they could do to him. He had turned evil.

At the ceremony there was an old woman
who was taking care of her two grandchildren, a boy and a girl.

When the eagle appeared, she cried out, "Don't touch it! It is a punishment! Let it go!
I've never seen one of these animals attack people."

But the others said, "Bring the hide. This eagle has come looking for his death."

As is the custom, they laid a skin on the ground
and the eagle, who was Rawi'jawi, sat on it,
though he didn't need to be tied as the eagle usually did.
He sat there voluntarily while, as is the custom when an eagle is sacrificed,
they covered him with gifts of seeds, grains,
and everything they could offer, until only his head was visible.

Knowing what was coming, the old woman took her grandchildren and left quickly
saying she couldn't bear to watch.

When the marksman shot an arrow into the eagle's head, everyone fell dead.

"They were happy and I was suffering," said Rawi'jawi as he flew away,
leaving the dead behind.

When Meadowlark arrived and saw what had happened,
he immediately flew off to tell Stagbuck,
who was the captain of Malibu
and all the villages as far as San Fernando and maybe farther.
He was the greatest of all the doctors.

Stagbuck knew Meadowlark's call meant someone was coming,
so he went down to the coast to meet Rawi'jawi
who was traveling up that way.

When they met, Stagbuck said, "What are you doing?
Do you think you're going to murder all the people here?"

"It's none of your business," said Rawi'jawi.

"You don't know who you are talking to," said Stagbuck. "Turn around."

Rawi'jawi did what he was told, and when he turned back,
he saw that standing in front of him was Stagbuck.
the greatest of them all.

Immediately he begged Stagbuck to pardon him.

Stagbuck agreed but cautioned him to stop what he was doing;
in fact, from then on, he must do nothing.

Rawi'jawi returned to the mountains behind Tujunga, sat down,
and turned to stone beside his wife.

They are still seated there,
two stones facing the village.

6   White People

26

The site of the village of Cahuenga beside the Los Angeles River; ritual
artifacts were found during road construction in 1935: Studio City.

October 8, 1542: Three Spanish ships, sailing north from Mexico seek a new route to the Spice Islands. As his ships pass the cliffs of San Pedro Bay, the Captain, Juan Rogriquez Cabrillo, writes in his journal: "The Bay of Smokes." When he lands on Santa Catalina Island (Pimu) at Avalon Harbor before sailing north, he logs brief descriptions of the landscape and natives.

Los Angeles enters Western history.

1565: The Manila Galleon, sent by Spain to the spice trade in the Philippines, sails yearly past San Clemente and Santa Catalina Islands.

1602: Sebastian Vizcaino lands at Isthmus Cove on Santa Catalina Island. Soldiers find the Indian's sacred enclosure, and, with their blunderbusses, shoot the two ravens who perch there. The people are shocked and grief stricken.

One day white people, walking or riding horses,
              passed by the villages around Palm Springs.
For awhile people called the first ones who arrived "Clever Men."
        Later more white people arrived by sailboat.
              Some people on the coast called them "People of the Sea."

The people around Palm Springs explained the arrival of white people this way:

While Mukat was holding up the sky during the battle with his twin brother,
             some of his children came to life while it was still dark
                and ran away to the north.
These are the White People.

In the beginning, when the sun finally appeared,
        its sudden brightness scared everyone,
         and they began chattering in languages Mukat couldn't understand.

Listening carefully, he found the one man
      who spoke the language of the people around Palm Springs
            and brought this man to his side.

This was the beginning of the Cahuilla people and their language.
This man now lives in the world of the evening star, moon, and sun.

Mukat let all the rest of the people move to other places.

Left behind among the Cahuilla people
      was one red-haired man with a white face
         who never sat still and was always crying and complaining
            like a cranky child.

      Mukat fixed a long stick between his legs
      and put a short stick, like a whip, in his hand.

      The man kept running around and around and around
      until one day he disappeared to the north,
         where he joined the other White People.

That night, Mukat brought his children into the Big House
      where their ceremonies would be held.
When they had settled themselves,
      the people asked him about a light they saw
        glowing in the north.

Mukat said it was their older and younger brothers
      and their older and younger sisters,
         the White People,
      the ones who had left at night.

Mukat said, "They did not hear me.
      They did not ask me.
         They are harmful spirits. They have four names."

EPILOGUE ❧ *Chinigchinich, the Spanish, the Yankees*

27

The site of the village of Yanga, now downtown Los Angeles, viewed
from the hill where, on August 2, 1769, the Gaspar de Portola expedition
camped near the North Broadway Bridge: Elysian Park.

1769: Gaspar de Portolá's overland expedition from San Diego to San Francisco in search of Monterey Bay.

Camping one evening near the Los Angeles River, a member of the expedition, Father Juan Crespí, records in his diary that it is a "full sized, full flowing river," "well lined with large trees, sycamores, willows, cottonwoods, and very large live oaks." He names the river Porciúncula (small portion) after a chapel in Italy important to the Franciscans, called Our Lady of the Angels.

Traveling with Portola is Father Junípero Serra, who founds missions from San Diego to San Francisco. These missions will secure California for the Spanish crown, souls for Rome, and provisions for the Manila Galleon on route to the Philippines for the spice trade.

Indian children are captured and baptized; distraught, their parents follow them to the mission.

Rape, influenza, dysentery, flogging, small pox,
                                    syphilis, tuberculosis, slave labor.
Deaths double the number of births.
Life expectancy at birth: 6.4 years.

                    Entire villages die from new diseases.
                                    The old songs don't heal them.
                Farming and herds of sheep and cattle
                        destroy native foods and sacred places.
            People around Los Angeles
                            begin to explain things this way:

Many ages the after the death of Wiyot,
                        a new spirit appeared:
                            Chinigchinich.

        Though most people say that he was born in Povunga,

some say that knowledge of Chinigchinich
was brought to the people around Los Angeles
from Pimu (Catalina Island).

Other people say this knowledge came from Santa Cruz Island.

He appeared when the First People were gathered in a council
at the village of Povunga, near Long Beach.

It happened long ago, when they were discussing the problem
of gathering food and eating
since white clay no longer nourished them.

While they were talking, a spirit startled them.
For several days it shone and retreated,
arrived and disappeared,
darting in one direction and then another.

Finally they called it into their circle to question it:

"Are you Wiyot?"

The spirit answered: "I am not Wiyot.
I am Chinigchinich.
I am more powerful than Wiyot.
I was born here at Povunga.
I live in the sky world.
As soon as I was born, I spoke. But my voice and my shape terrified the First People.
This is why Tamaiyowit, my mother, hid me until I was grown.
Since then I have remained invisible."

Some people say Chinigchinich was born in the North
and named Oiamot.
Others say his mother was Auzar
and his father was the comet Tacu,
who some people call the cannibal Takwish.
Some say he came from the stars.

All agree that he is dangerous,
respectable, powerful, sacred, and wise.

Chinigchinish, invisible and all seeing, secretive and strict,
came with the knowledge-power

needed to save the people from disastrous epidemics
and the rule of the White People.

Anyone who serves him, keeps his secrets, and shares his power—
doctors, rocks, wind, animals, plants, baskets for offerings, datura—
is called by his name.

One day, near Santa Ana, a boy was out hunting
rabbits and quail with his bow and arrows. A rabbit
he was after jumped down a hole. So the boy used
a stick to poke around in it to see if the rabbit was
hiding there. He could feel the rabbit, so he kept
digging. As he dug he found things he wanted to
take to his mother and sister.

He dug so deep that he arrived at the place where
the Chinigchinich were living. They greeted him,
welcomed him to sit down, and built a huge fire.
The boy was afraid and didn't know what to do.

One at a time, the Chinigchinich stood up and
began leaping around the fire, whirling and dancing
with lots of big motions. They each danced into
the fire and stood in the middle of it with flames
burning around their heads. Then they turned to the
boy and said, "It's your turn now."

Terrified, he sang a song and then leapt in. As he
stood there, he felt no heat and when he walked out
without a mark, they all shouted, "Now you are a
good Chinigchinich!"

Before Chinigchinich everyone used to dance in a
quieter way. Now people dance in this big way.
They still dance into the fire.

Chinigchinich asked them, "What are you talking about in your council?"

The First People answered: "Our captain, Wiyot, has died.
Now we must eat something besides white clay.
We are discussing how to do this."

Chinigchinich said, "I will give you the power to become what you dream of eating."
Pointing to each one, he said:

"To you I give the power to sing rain.
To you the power to sing dew.
To you the power to sing acorns.
To you the power to sing rabbits.
To you the power to sing ducks.
To you the power to sing geese.
To you the power to sing deer."

The new spirit, Chinigchinich,
transformed the First People into the world of weather, food, and sacred objects.

From Povunga, Chinigchinich traveled to Lake Elsinore where he gathered clay
and shaped it into human beings, male and female.

When he named his creation, the new people came to life.

Gathering the new people in a council, he instructed them about
the laws they would obey,
the circular ceremonial enclosure they would build,
and the ceremonies they would perform.

He warned them that if they didn't perform these actions
correctly,
he would kill them with bad luck, sickness,
or punishment by his avengers
who prick, poison, or bite.

He said that by strictly following his rules, by properly using their knowledge-power,
the people's lives and the life of the land
would be restored to balance, the hungry would be fed,
and all sicknesses, even the new ones, would be cured.

Chingichnich told them that whenever he gave them what they needed,
they were to give him thanks.

He said, though they would never see him, he would watch them.
He would travel around the whole world,
watching everything,

knowing everything,
            even private thoughts kept in their hearts.

He said, "My avengers are all Chinigchinich and sacred to me:"

Raven, who is the sky, and whose beak and talons you will carry in the ceremonial
            quiver made of bobcat or young coyote skin.
            It is filled with arrows and hung in the sacred enclosure.

Raven is my messenger and my spy.
            He will shoot anyone who breaks my laws.
            His crystal tipped arrows dive deep into the body
                        causing sickness, even death.

He will talk to those who know his language,
                        telling them who is coming
                        and what is about to happen.

Bald Eagle, whose beak and talons you will carry in the ceremonial quiver.

Bear, who will bite and whose claws you will carry in the ceremonial quiver.

Mountain Lion, who will bite and whose claws you will carry
            in the ceremonial quiver.

Deer, whose horns you will carry in the ceremonial quiver.

Rattlesnake, who will bite, who comes in many colors,
                        who may be invisible,
                        who will strike in any direction,
                        who might travel at night,
                        who will live near the springs you will visit
                                    when you hunt in the mountains.

Stingray, who stings like a knife.

Tarantula Wasp, who stings.

Black Widow Spider, whose bite can kill you.

And these are also my avengers and sacred to me:

Garden Spider
Tarantula
Trapdoor Spider
Scorpion
Tick
Centipede.

And these whom you cannot see are sacred to me:
Red Deer, who is huge with immense spreading antlers.
He will stand still for you until you shoot and miss.
Fleeing and halting, he will lead you
to rattlesnakes
or hidden cliffs.
The One Who Lives Underground in the Mountains,
growling and shaking the stones.
The Ferocious Giant Water Insect
The One Who Throws You Down
The One Who Breaks You.

And these plants are sacred to me:
Datura
Sage
Tobacco
Rose and Blackberry
Stick of Wood That Can Cause Death.

And these crystals are sacred to me:
Amethysts
Clear and white quartz, especially the large ones.

There are three kinds of crystals:

Those that cure. Only doctors will touch them.

Those worn in hairpins and jewelry
for their beauty and for protection.

Ordinary crystals used as drills.

Pink, Green, or Black Tourmaline that tip Raven's arrows.

Doctors rub this crystal on people
punished by Chinigchinich.

These minerals are sacred to me:

> *Noot* (captain stone): The stone that whistles when it feels neglected.
> > It has many powers.
> > Ground to a powder and rubbed on the legs,
> > > it makes a runner fast and strong.

> *Tôshaawt*: The small iron-rich stone from the islands
> > used to bring rain and to heal.

These ceremonial objects are sacred to me:

> The ceremonial mortar
> > from which the boys drink Manit when they are initiated
> The tray basket where offerings of grain and pipes are placed
> Feather skirt made of golden eagle, bald eagle, or condor feathers
> > and all headdresses and objects used in my ceremonies.

Before Chingichnich appeared to the First People,
> when he had not yet revealed himself,
he called himself Saor, a common person who does not know how to dance,
> who is not yet initiated.
When he danced before the people, like Toovit: the first Person to sing,
> he called himself Tobet. He wore the sacred feather skirt and headdress
> and he painted his body black and red.

After dancing for a long time, he initiated certain people,
> teaching them how to be captains and doctors.

> Each new initiate was sworn to secrecy.

> He taught them how to prepare the datura with salt water and tobacco
> > and how to drink it for visions,
> > protection against bear and snake bites,
> > and for healing.

> He taught them how to give it to boys during their initiation.
> He taught them the guidelines by which they must live
> > and to teach these rules to the new initiates,
> > boys and girls, as they study the ground painting.

> Pointing to the painting,
> > the elders say to the boys:

Do you see this? This is bear-panther.
They will catch you and kill you
        if you do not respect your elder relatives and all grown ups.

If you believe, everyone will know your goodness
      and you will kill bear-panther.

This earth hears you; the sky and wood-mountain see you.
Raven's arrows may strike you dead
        if you don't follow our ways.
But if you believe, if you honor our path,
      you will gain fame and be praised.
Everyone will know your name.
They will ask: Whose son is he?

You will grow old to counsel your own sons and daughters.

     Do not secretly eat food left over from dinner.
     Do not be angry when you eat.
     Do not be angry at your elder relatives.

When hunting and you kill a rabbit or a deer
       and an old man asks you for it,
    hand it to him at once.
Don't be angry when you give it—and don't throw it at him.
When he goes home, he will praise you,
        and you will kill many more.
Your bow shot will be straight.

This is a rattlesnake. It will kill you.
    Do not shout when old people are nearby.
    When old people visit your house, welcome them.
    Offer them food and water at once.
    If you have none, then tell them so politely.
If you do this, and a rattlesnake should bite you, you will arrive home.
But if you are wicked, you will not arrive.
People will say that your wickedness is why you were bitten.

See this? This is black widow spider and it will bite you.
    Do not approach your wife when she is menstruating.
    Bathe every morning before dawn.
    Be active. Don't be phony.
    Don't eat too much or you will grow heavy
        and get tired when you run.

If you do these things, you will not be stung,
    you will not go blind,
        you will not die of consumption and the blood-vomiting sickness.
These will all pass by you.

        If you heed this speech spoken by the Ancestors,
    you will grow old and counsel your sons and daughters
            like these old people sitting here with you.

        And when you die, people will know about it.
        They will shout three times, sending your spirit
            to Towish—The Milky Way—
                to join the stars, moon, and sun.

    Pointing to the ground painting,
    the elders say to the girl:
            Do you see all these? If you do not believe,
            they are going to kill you.

                Don't be careless.
                Don't be phony.
                Don't be stingy.
                Don't look sideways.

You must not receive a person in your house with anger.
Welcome your elder relatives and your in-laws when they come to your home.
When you visit them in their homes, they will speak well of you
        and welcome you politely.

Do not eat food left over from dinner or, when you have a baby, it will be sick,
        your stomach will swell, and your eyes will granulate.
You will drink hot water when you menstruate
        and bitter herbs when you are pregnant.
                These will cleanse you
                    so you will give birth quickly.

After your initiation, use only a stick to scratch yourself and not your hands.
If you scratch yourself with your hands, you will have pimples.

You will bathe every morning before dawn.
        If you do this, your hair will grow long,
                you will not feel the cold,
                    and you will grow fat.
Remember to paint yourself so people will see you.

If you heed this speech spoken by the Ancestors,
you will grow old and counsel your sons and daughters
like these old people sitting here with you.

And when you die, people will know about it.
They will shout three times, sending your spirit
to Towish—The Milky Way—
to join the stars, moon, and sun.

One day, after teaching about initiation,
as Chinigchinich danced for the people,
dressed and painted as Tobet,
he rose up among the stars.

Arisen, he called himself Quaguar.
Some people won't mention this name
and call him Giver of Life.
Other people say that when Chinigchinich died, he passed into the Other World,
the Above and Below,
residing among the stars
to watch over and guide his people.

Along trade routes and trails, from the coast to the mountains to the deserts,
word spread quickly about Chinigchinich and his new ways
that would defend and enforce the people's knowledge-power.

Knowing that power can be learned,
some doctors study
the language of the white people
and their religion,
hoping this knowledge
will give them powers
to heal and protect their people
from the new diseases.

If they strengthen themselves, said Chinigchinich,
guard the power in the ceremonies by doing them exactly,

and live strictly according to what they now know to be true,
they could stop the new diseases
and restore the landscape and the sacred places.

1775:   Hundreds of warriors from many villages burn down Mission San Diego.

1778:   At Mission San Juan Capistrano, three villages revolt protesting rapes, murders,
and the destruction of native crops caused by drought and the suppression of their
rituals. Unless the doctors can do their work, the people know the drought will
continue and they will starve.

1779:   A revolt at Mission San Gabriel is led by a neophyte known as Nicolás José, a
Tongva (Gabrielino) man from Shevaanga, a village near the mission.

1781:   Eleven families arrive from Mexico to found El Pueblo de Nuestra Señora la
Reina de los Angeles del Rio de Porciúncula (The Village of Our Lady Queen of
the Angels) near the wild grape and rose tangled banks of the Los Angeles River,
named by Portolá El Rio Porciúncula. The new pueblo is established near a large
village called Yanga, "Place Where the Earth is Salty." These newly arrived men,
women and children are Black, Mulatto, Mestizo, and Indian.

1785:   Toypurina, a twenty-seven-year-old doctor and captain's daughter from the
mountain village of Hapchinga, inspires leaders from seven villages to follow her
in attacking Mission San Gabriel. She promises that she will use her power to kill
the soldiers, who will be dead when they attack. A convert finds out about the
plan and warns the missionaries. Soldiers repel the attack and capture its leaders,
including Toypurina and Nicolas José.

1801:   When epidemics kill hundreds of people, a Chumash woman doctor announces
a vision: The people must be re-baptized in the name of the Earth Mother, Shup,
and perform rituals for her, or they would all die. Her teachings are linked with
Chinigchinich and spread widely.

1810:   Eight hundred warriors from many villages revolt against Mission San Gabriel,
protesting rapes and the destruction of the land and sacred places. The Indians
are defeated: lashings, children removed from families and taken to the Mission,
forced baptisms, prison sentences, forced labor.

1821:   Mexico declares independence from Spain. Mission lands and Indian laborers are
released for private ownership and use.

Trees, shrubs, and plants hacked to make grazing land
for Spanish sheep and cattle
that eat the edible roots,
seeds, and seedlings,
destroying the food supply
and trampling sacred places.

The sheep and cattle eat the native bunch grass
to its roots
and the bunch grass fails.
Water, not held by those thick matted roots,
washes away:
fewer springs and streams.

1823:   In mid-December, during the season of the sun's return to his southern house and
the Winter Solstice ceremonies, a comet appears in the north. By February, its
tail splits in two, one part streaming toward the sun and the other away from it.

Comets are the hearts of great captains and doctors
who have died and then return
to give the people important messages.

Comets appear like stars
wearing the sacred headband,
the spirit net which is the Milky Way.

Chinigchinich teaches that human hair
holds the spirit.
It is woven into ceremonial nets, ropes
and the headbands of captains,
doctors, and dancers.

1824:   In February, Chumash warriors, some wearing headbands of woven human hair,
attack Mission Santa Barbara and burn down Mission Santa Inés. Many Indians
are killed. It is the largest revolt against the Missions.

Warriors who wear the hair headbands say,
"If they shoot at me, water will come out of the cannon.
If they shoot at me,
the bullet will not enter my flesh."

1825:   From September until November, a comet sailing toward the northwest appears in the
        southeastern sky.

                    Around San Juan Capistrano captains and doctors
                            gather to discuss what caused
                                the appearance of the comets.

                    They decide that the comets
                                signal very serious changes to come.

                    Others say this new comet is Sirout,
                                who, for the people around Los Angeles,
                                    is the father of Wiyot.
                    Since he always brings happiness
                                and everything they needed to live well,
                            the comet must mean
                    they are soon going to return to their way of life.

                    Many believe it is Tacu, the father of Chinigchinich.

                    Some say that the comets mean
                                they will soon be free to live however they please.
                    Even if they continue to live at the missions,
                            they won't be subjected to anyone,
                                            Spanish or Indian.

                    The eldest among them disagree,
                                saying that Sirout had come to warn them
                            about another people
                    who will soon arrive
                            and who will treat them as slaves,
                                    causing starvation and suffering.
                    Sirout appeared to urge them to escape
                                    the coming devastation.

1842:   While looking for wild onions in Placerita Canyon near Newhall, Francisco Lopez
        finds gold under an oak tree. It is named "Oak of Golden Dreams."

1848:   War, broken out two years earlier, ends between the United States and Mexico. The
        Californios are defeated. The Treaty of Guadalupe Hidalgo assigns Los Angeles along
        with California and all the land north of the Rio Grande—half of Mexico—to the
        United States.

Gold is discovered in the small town of Coloma near Sacramento. Gold Rush!

1849:   Yankees pour into Northern and Southern California.

1850:   California joins the Union as the 31st state.

1854:   Smallpox wipes out more Indian laborers. Chinese peasants arrive to replace them.

Los Angeles: a Yankee,
              Spanish,
              African American,
              Chinese,
              Native American city.

1860:   William Henry Brewer leads the first California Geological Survey as its field director,
         recording plants and weather, and mapping geological features. The Boundary
         Commission's men chart the borders of the state of California.

1917:   Indian people in the San Fernando Valley say that around Castle Peak,
                    down in a dry well,
                          there are seven stones sitting in a circle.

        These are the Ancestors, the Old Ones, the Seven Viejos.

At that time people would toss chia seeds and other offerings to them.
They did this to be sure there would be a good seed and acorn harvest the next year.

Whenever they pounded seeds or acorns into flour in their mortars,
                    they always threw the final handful into the cooking fire.

This was for the Seven Viejos.

One evening in Calabasas, a town near Castle Peak,
                    three people sat around the kitchen table
                                        talking about their beliefs:
                    the man whose house it was,
                    his old mother-in-law,
                              who had converted at Mission San Gabriel,
                    and a friend.

28
Leonis Adobe: Calabasas.

They were discussing whether or not the Seven Old Ones were gone,
                  now that the White People had come with their new religion.

The friend said that one time, when he was out hunting on Anacapa or Santa Rosa,
          he couldn't remember which island it was,
                    he and his companions came upon a deep hole.

They peered into it
        and saw the Seven Viejos at the bottom
           sitting in a circle
              with their shoulders hunched and their heads bent down.
Despite all the changes, all the destruction, the Ancestors were still here.

Right away they threw what they had,
             clothes and food,
                down to them as offerings.

"When I die, I'm going away with the Seven Old Ones," the friend said.

The man laughed saying he didn't know how it was possible
          to have two beliefs at the same time, Catholic and Indian.

His old mother-in-law spoke up and said it certainly was.
Moving her fingers along side by side,
            one then the other across the table,
              she said, "Where one fails, the other helps."

 *Postscript*

29
Los Angeles at night.

2009:   One night Raven and Coyote are sitting in the mountains beside the Hollywood
         sign looking over the city.

         "Look at all those lights," says Raven, cocking one eye then the other as he
studies the sight. "They just keep spreading. It's like a wildfire down there."

Coyote gets real excited by all the twinkling, and he says to Raven:
         "Don't you know what they're doing? They're wiring the stars to the ground.
         They're trying to make Heaven on Earth!"

(He laughs because he thinks he's funny and, anyway, it's night and he likes the heat.)

Raven sighs:
         "Well, if they'd leave a few of those stars in the sky,
                            they could see that it already is."

The Sacred Sites project evolved over more than two decades. Each time I picked up the trail, I was supported and encouraged by Native Americans, scholars, libraries, schools, universities, art institutions, family, and friends. I am concerned, therefore, that I might forget some of those who contributed to its creation. So, first let me acknowledge that the efforts of many people and institutions are woven into the pages of this book; it could not have been written without their significant and generous support. I am deeply thankful to all who joined me in discovering Southern California's venerable character and its ancient and remarkable history.

My appreciation of the landscape was incalculably deepened by the Native American people who have guided my journey, especially Anthony Morales, chief of the Gabrielino-Tongva Tribal Council; the late Vera Rocha; Angie Behrens, chair of the Gabrielino-Tongva Springs Foundation; and the Acjachemen (Juaneño) leaders Rebecca Robles and Rhonda Robles. I am immensely grateful for all they have shown me.

Though I was born in Los Angeles, when I returned here in the mid-1980s I realized how little I knew about the region. Three people planted the seeds that led me to write a grant proposal for a performance that would investigate the geographic and ethnographic prehistory of Santa Monica, where I live. When I was an undergraduate at the University of Arizona, the late Byrd Granger, professor of English and folklore, introduced me to the study of mythology and to Southwestern in-

digenous cultures. Poet Thomas Crowe shared with me his work helping to save Cherokee sacred sites in North Carolina. Poet Gary Snyder inspired me with his story about how, when he first moved to Kyoto, Japan, he made a pilgrimage to the local mountain shrines to introduce himself. Thereafter, he said, he felt at home. I determined to give this a try in Los Angeles. Additionally, Snyder's poem, "What Happened Here Before," served as both template and inspiration for this work.

In 1986 my proposal to create *Sacred Sites/Santa Monica* was funded by the Santa Monica Arts Commission and the Santa Monica Arts Foundation. Without their initial support, this project never would have come to life. (The cast included Bob Lake, Mike Rick, Catherine Theobald, and myself, with director Ric Montejano, designer Shan Weaver, and musician Bruce Glover.) Subsequent funding from the Santa Monica School District and the Santa Monica College Associated Students and Continuing Education Program provided for further evolution of the work by funding performances and student workshops. During this time Kathy Gronau joined the project as a fundraiser, friend, and all-around supporter, a role she continues to this day. Paul O'Lague, a professor of cell biology at UCLA with a gift for clearly explaining complex scientific concepts and discoveries, became an indispensable guide and resource through the span of this project. Elina O'Lague generously provided me with a studio in the attic of her restaurant, Warszawa.

In 1992 Susan Mason guided a revision of the script and directed a new series of performances, *Sacred Sites/Los Angeles*, as part of a Ford Foundation–funded project at California State University at Los Angeles's Department of Theatre Arts and Dance. (The cast included Felipe Galvez, Gina Honda, Akeime Mitterlehner, and Erica Ortega, with music by Craig Kupka.) I am grateful to faculty from USC's Center for the Study of Los Angeles and the Geography Department, members of Friends of the Los Angeles River, and the late Tongva leader Vera Rocha, who led post-performance discussions.

An important transition came when I was invited to present the material solo for the second-grade class at PS1 school in Santa Monica. Subsequently, when Andrew Beath, founder of Earth Trust Foundation, invited me to give a lecture about my work, instead I presented an early version of what later became my one-woman performance based on *Sacred Sites/Los Angeles*. I am grateful to Beath's assistants at that time, Shiva Rea and especially Valerie Fowler, a long-time friend and supporter of this project. Eventually the piece evolved into a full-on performance (with director Zoey Zimmerman, musician David Koff, and with assistance on set design and construction from Bill Kasper). I first presented this work in 1997 at Nature's Workshop: Environmental Change in Twentieth-Century Southern California, an interdisciplinary conference held at California State University at Northridge.

I am grateful to all those who invited me to perform or to lead Sacred Sites tours for their schools, cultural centers, and universities, especially the Lila Wallace–Readers Digest Literary Series at Nevada County's North Columbia Cultural Center; Crossroads School in Santa Monica; and the USC Fine Arts Department. Jeannette Hope and Julie Drew sponsored my performance at an Australian Women in Archaeology conference, Betty Bernhard at Pomona College, and Jeff Dean at Ohlone College. I am particularly grateful to Miriyam Glazer at the University of Judaism and Phoebe Ozuna at Roosevelt High School, both of whom invited me to give performances, presentations, and tours over several years. The enthusiasm of these diverse audiences encouraged me to continue with the project.

In 1998 I received an International Artist Grant from the 18th Street Art Center to perform *Sacred Sites/Los Angeles* at the University of Utrecht in the Netherlands. I am grateful to Jan Williamson and Clayton Campbell, then co-directors of the center, for this award. At the University of Utrecht, Eugene van Erven, my sponsor and now friend, and his family looked after me with utmost care. I am most gratefully indebted to the accomplished and delightful Birgit Spoon, who assisted me with the performances.

When I first sat down to create these scripts, I thought I would simply consult books already written about the Southern California landscape and indigenous cultures. But the books I needed hadn't been written. Not even Bill McCawley's indispensable *The First Angelinos* was yet in print. Thus I began a journey of discovery that continues to enthrall me.

Archaeologist Clay Singer got me started studying Southern California's indigenous history. He led me to archaeologist Chester King, who became a mainstay in my research and who has taken me on many unforgettable fieldtrips to rock art, village, and ceremonial sites, and other remarkable locations. Under Chester's guidance I began to see Southern California through another cultural lens. Bill McCawley provided important guidance early in the project. Tom Blackburn also supported my research with his scholarly acumen and personal enthusiasm. He led me to Lowell Bean, whose work is central to Southern California indigenous studies and whose influence on my work is immeasurable.

Other archaeologists, ethnographers, and historians who provided encouragement and contributed to my understanding of indigenous cultures and the workings of his-

tory include: the late John Romani, the late
Gwen Romani, Dan Larson, Paul Apodaca,
the late Roy Salls, the late William Wallace,
Michael Kuhn, Bob Edberg, the late Charles
Rozaire, the late Clement Meighan, Margaret
Miles, John Johnson, Edward Krupp, and Steve
Schwartz. I consulted with linguists Pam
Munro and the late Bill Bright when I first be-
gan reading indigenous literatures.

When I set out to understand the Southern California landscape, I spent hours talking
with George Jefferson, who was at that time
the George C. Page Museum Associate Curator, and Santa Monica College geography professor Bill Selby. Years later, when I became
determined to transform my scripts into a
book, I turned to my friend and colleague,
geographer John Cloud, who directed me to
the paleogelogists and paleobotanists I needed to meet. He also introduced me to car-
tographer Michael Hermann, who patiently
worked with me through several drafts as we
crafted a map of Southern California.

I am deeply indebted to the late geologist
Peter Weigand, professor of geology at California State University at Northridge, who
spent many hours guiding me through the
layers of West Coast paleogeology. Whenever I turn to this material I am reminded of
his generosity and the memorable fieldtrip we
took into the San Gabriel Mountains where
it all came alive for me. He, along with geologist Eugene Fritsche, provided the patient
guidance I needed to understand the complex
and dynamic structures that underlie Southern California. Since there were no books
written for the general public about this topic,
they and their colleague George Dunne talked with me at length and reviewed my work
as it progressed. I am also grateful to Ray Ingersoll, geology professor at UCLA, who added significantly to my understanding of how
Southern California took shape.

I am grateful to Bruce Tiffney, David
Whistler, Roy van der Hoek, Lindsey Groves,
Chris Shaw, and John Iwerks, who introduced
me to the exotic array of life forms that have
called Southern California home. Larry Barnes
guided me through layers of Southern California prehistory and introduced me to the collections of the Los Angeles County Museum of
Natural History.

Many thanks to Peg Brady at the Southwest
Museum, and to the librarians and collections
directors at the Southwest Museum's Braun
Research Library; to the Huntington Free Library in New York City (whose Native American collection is now at Cornell University);
to the American Museum of Natural History;
to the Los Angeles County Museum of Natural History; to the UCLA Archaeological Survey; to the George C. Page Museum; to the
Santa Monica City Library; to the Bancroft Library; to UC Riverside's Tomás Rivera
Library; and to UCLA's Charles E. Young
Research Library. Thanks as well to Merrilee
Fellows, NASA's Manager for Community In-
volvement for Environmental Remediation.

Over the course of its evolution this manuscript not only traversed the territory of peer
review, it was also critiqued for felicity and accu-
racy by a generous and helpful group of readers that included Steve Goldman, Bronwen Sen-
nish, Dale Pendell, Rhonda Robles, and many
of the scientists I consulted. I offer my heartfelt
appreciation to the members of Writers' Circle,
who provided regular encouragement and cri-
tiques: Chris Ferris, Deborah Bogen, Fran Whit-
ner, Carroll Hodge, Marcia Hanscom, and De-
idre Gainor. And I am also deeply thankful to
the members of the Woman's Lunch Group
for their wholehearted support over the many
years I've worked on this project: Susan Che-
hak, Jo Giese, Jo Ann Matyas, Luchita Mullican,
Virginia Mullin, Maria Munroe, Doreen Nelson,
Amanda Pope, Janet Sternburg, Carol Tavris,
Carolyn See, and especially Judith Searle, who
taught me how to write a book proposal early
on in this adventure.

Friends, assistants, and fellow artists contributed many kinds of sustenance and inspiration. Doron Yitzchaki, Joshua Cohen, LaTo-

sha Traylor, and Lola Terrell assisted me in organizing a plethora of files and books. Others whose love, support, and good ideas kept my work on track include Ellen Graff, Cynthia Lester, Gayle Kimball, Teddy Emrich, Ruth Ghio, Laura Pendell, Carmen Ketola, Allaire Koslo, Sue Dakin, Michael Barnard, the late Merle Pendell, Brenda Goodman, Jennifer Penton, Francis DellaVecchia, Michael Dawson, Linda Vallejo, Bruce Kijewski, Michael O'Keefe, Thomas Suriya, Malcolm Margolin, Donna Gregory, Jane Anne Jeffries, the late Brian McClellan, Basia Kenton, Sharmagne Leland-St. John, Michael Attie, Martha Bardak, Michael Stout, Virginia Stout, Peggy Watson, and Sharon Sekhon, director of the Studio for Southern California History. My thanks to the English Department at East Los Angeles College, where I teach, and especially to my department chair, James Kenny. Phyllis Faber encouraged me when I was flagging and guided me through the task of finding a publisher. I also thank my attorney, Jonathan Kirsch, for his guidance. And I offer deep appreciation to my Dharma teachers, Robert Aitken and Joko Beck.

David Mueller introduced me to Jonathan Spaulding, vice president of exhibitions at the Autry National Center of the American West, who supported this project. The Autry Center provided funding for the photography included in this book. Through historian Bill Deverell I met Matt Bokovoy, my superb editor at University of Nebraska Press who, along with his assistant, Elisabeth Chretien, has been an excellent guide through the publishing process. It's been a joyous adventure traveling with photographer Juergen Nogai to the sites that are at the center of this story. Juergen's wife, artist Jeannie Winston Nogai, generously lent her excellent eye to our work. I especially appreciate the Ballona Institute's support and Deirdre Gainor's steady friendship and insightful guidance. I am deeply thankful for Wellford Wilms's generous encouragement, which included listening to me read the manuscript out loud through many drafts and providing me with a secluded cottage in which to write.

My parents and maternal grandparents, who moved to Southern California from New Mexico in the late 1930s and told stories about the paradise they found here, inspired my love for the landscape, especially the high desert of the Antelope Valley and the ocean that was so important to my father. Finally, I am most grateful to my son, Sean Daughtry, and my daughter, Califia Suntree, who shared with me the many years I spent on the trail of this project. I am especially indebted to Califia who, with her extraordinary editorial skills, honed this manuscript with expertise, honesty, and kindness.

The following people reviewed this book in preparation for its paperback publication. I am most grateful for their scrutiny and suggestions: Robert M. de Groot, PhD, ShakeAlert National Coordinator for Communication, Education, and Outreach, USGS; Raymond V. Ingersoll, PhD, professor of geology (emeritus), University of California, Los Angeles; John R. Johnson, PhD, curator of anthropology, Santa Barbara Museum of Natural History; and Paul O'Lague, PhD, Department of Molecular, Cell, and Developmental Biology (retired), UCLA.

Notes

BOOK ONE: WESTERN SCIENCE

1. Light, Space, Matter

5   **14 Billion Years Ago:** The current date given for the Big Bang, which birthed our universe, is between 12 and 14 billion years ago. However, the possibility that there might exist parallel or multiple simultaneous universes, as proposed by some cosmologists, adds intrigue to the usual proposal that there is only one universe begun with only one Big Bang.

5   **or the spectral harmonics:** Science writer K. C. Cole elucidates contemporary physics, including string theory, in *The Hole in the Universe*. Physicist Brian Greene, a leading proponent of string theory, presents a reader-friendly introduction and tells the compelling story of its evolution in *The Elegant Universe*.

6   **doubling its size in seconds:** Describing the unfolding of the universe as it expands in terms of seconds or minutes is essentially metaphorical. See T. Padmanabhan's *After the First Three Minutes* and John Gribben's *The Birth of Time*.

10   **From one proton:** The formation of carbon, and thereby life on Earth, is considered to be one of the universe's more remarkable phenomena. John Gribben and Martin Rees, in *Cosmic Coincidences*, tell the improbable story of carbon and the role played by British astronomer Fred Hoyle in its discovery. Hoyle famously rejected the theory of the Big Bang even though he had coined the term.

2. Galaxy, Planet, Moon, Rain

19   **The pole reversals:** The relationship between pole reversals and the discovery of plate tectonics is a story of adventure and intellectual daring. For an introduction see Dan McKenzie's "Seafloor Magnetism and Drifting Continents" in *A Century of Nature*, edited by Laura Garwin and Tim Lincoln.

3. Wandering North America, Life, Death

27   **Perhaps in pond scum:** There are many theories about the origins of life and where this astounding event may have occurred. See biochemist and Nobel laureate Christian de Duve's *Vital Dust* and geologist Richard Cowan's bestselling and eminently readable textbook, *History of Life*.

31   **Thin and flat:** According to Peter Cattermole, in *Building Planet Earth*, the core of North America has been stable for at least two billion years.

42   **coal:** Ironically, by burning coal as fuel we appear to be returning the earth's climate to the conditions prevailing when it was first laid down in its beds.

4. Reptiles, Flowers, Mammals, Rivers

64   **The Juan de Fuca:** The ongoing subduction of the Farallon Plate is responsible for the magnificent and, in some cases, still active volcanic peaks of the Pacific Northwest.

5. Southern California Coming: Mountains in Motion

79   **All swimming, feeding, dying:** In 1998 the Geology Department at California State University at Northridge unveiled *MioScene*, a mural by plein-air painter John Iwerks. The painting depicts Southern California during the Miocene: volcanoes, the North River, animal life that surpasses the more familiar Ice Age fauna in variety and oddity, and the ocean rippling against the rising mountains.

91   **the Western and Eastern Transverse Ranges:** Most mountain ranges in North America run north and south.

6. Southern California Ice Age:
 Bountiful Homeland

97 **The Santa Clara River:** Running from Acton to the Pacific between Ventura and Oxnard, this is the last remaining wild, unchannelized, major river in Southern California and provides habitat, open space, and recreation. There are many archaeological sites along the Santa Clara's banks and the Sierra Club works continuously to preserve the river's wild status, which is regularly threatened by overdevelopment.

102 **condor:** Condors still sail over Southern California. Playful, curious, intelligent, social, and ancient, these magnificent birds struggle against the limitations imposed on them by urbanization, including our litter, lead in our bullets, and the antifreeze we dump. Contact the Ventana Wildlife Society to learn more about condor preservation.

103 **The Los Angeles River:** Blake Grumbecht's *The Los Angeles River* is an essential reference. Many people, especially the Friends of the Los Angeles River and The River Project, work to restore the river to its role as a central and enriching feature of the Southern California landscape.

105 **Amboy and Pisgah:** Robert Sharp and Allen Glazner's *Geology Underfoot in Southern California* provides excellent descriptions of the region's geology as well as maps and directions for outings to see such interesting features as these two volcanoes.

107 **collects in an underground lake:** The aquifer beneath the Los Angeles basin is comprised of underground reservoirs whose water would cover 110,000 acres 200 feet deep if taken all together, according to the Metropolitan Water District.

110 **The Ballona Wetlands:** In a region where 98 percent of coastal wetlands have been destroyed by development, 600 of Ballona's original 2,000 acres have been preserved. At the base of the Westchester bluffs, the wetlands' southern boundary, the largest indigenous cemetery ever discovered in Los Angeles was found in the path of a runoff channel for the Playa Vista development. Rather than reorient the channel, however, more than a thousand bodies were removed in buckets, the grave goods were retained, and the bodies were reburied elsewhere on the property. The Ballona Institute is an excellent resource for information and tours of the wetlands.

111 **Santarosae:** Formed when the sea level was nearly 300 feet lower than it is today, Santarosae was only six miles from the mainland, making it easy for the Columbian mammoth to swim across. In a smaller environment with no predators the fourteen-foot tall mammoth shrank to an average height of four to six feet at the shoulder and evolved into a new species: the Channel Island pygmy mammoth. Skeletons of these animals can be seen at the Santa Barbara Museum of Natural History and the Los Angeles County Museum of Natural History.

116 **people, in multiple migrations:** The story of how human beings came to the Americas is earnestly disputed. Dates of the arrival of the first people are regularly pushed back. Though the study of genetics has helped date the migrations from Siberia, the possibility that there were migrations from other regions is the topic of ongoing investigation.

In 1999 researchers from the Santa Barbara Museum of Natural History, with the aid of DNA testing, discovered that human bones found on Santa Rosa Island and previously dated at 10,000 years ago were in fact at least between 13,000 and 13,200 years ago. These remains, named Arlington Springs Man, are thus far the second-oldest human remains found in North America.

117 **a comet shatters:** In 2009 research emerged suggesting that a comet fragmented above North America and caused widespread fires and intense climate change. It also suggests that this catastrophe may have caused the disappearance of large Ice Age mammals, a major environmental transformation whose cause has been debated for years.

124 **Life, right here:** The names of the sacred landscape features are from the following tribal languages: Kas'élewun from Chumash; Iwinhinmu and Toshololo from Chumash; Hidakupa from Tongva; Juit gait from Tongva; Piwipwi from Tongva or Serrano; Jamiwo from Tongva; Xuungova from Tongva; Pimu from Tongva; Dume from Chumash; Asawtnga from Tongva.

131   **First there is:** I begin with the Quechnajuichom (Luiseño) origin story as told to Constance Goddard DuBois by Lucario Cuevish and Salvador Cuevas in 1908. The people named Luiseño by the Spanish (after Mission San Luis Rey de Francia) occupied the area approximately between Agua Hedionda in San Diego County in the south to San Onofre on the coast and extending north to Santiago Peak. Today the people call themselves the Quechnajuichom.

DuBois published her translation in an essay (in *American Archaeology and Ethnography*, vol. 8), but I drew primarily from her handwritten transcription of Cuevish's recitation in my attempt to appreciate his phrasing and diction. Cuevish, when blind and near death, recited from memory while DuBois, sitting next to her translator, wrote down his words as fast as she could. Many scholars consider his to be the least affected by European influences of all the versions of this myth. For me its poetic beauty, most evident in her original notes, sets it apart from all the other versions of this myth.

Constance Goddard DuBois was a bluestocking Connecticut novelist who, inspired by Helen Hunt Jackson, devoted a decade of her life to visiting, researching, collecting, and recording the cultures of Southern California's indigenous people (1897 to 1908), especially the Luiseño and Diegeño. DuBois spent considerable effort advocating and raising money for the people that were at that time known as the Mission Indians. Perhaps because she was a novelist, she recognized the important role played by myths and songs in understanding culture. While most archaeologists and anthropologists of her era were studying social systems and material culture like baskets, ritual objects, and tools, DuBois brought recording equipment by wagon to document the oral traditions of the indigenous people she came to know and deeply value.

The Quechnajuichom (Luiseño) creation myth is also recounted by Alfred Kroeber in his *Handbook of California Indians*; another version is found in John Peabody Harrington's notes on Father Gerónimo Boscana's *Chinigchinich*.

132   **He blows out his spirit breath:** A ceremonial groan or exhalation is used in rituals and in the recitation of sacred narratives to send the spirit, especially of someone who has died, to the Milky Way.

137   **they are united:** Sexual transgression, especially the seriously taboo act of incest, is part of the drama of many creation myths.

140   **Manit, The Vine That Can Talk:** Manit is the Tongva (Gabrielino) name for *Datura wrightii*. Early in the Mission era datura came to be known by the Nahuatl-derived name *toloache*. It is used throughout the Southwest and California for visions, clairvoyance, and many medical purposes. In Chumash mythology datura is personified as Momoy, an elderly, wealthy widow who sees the future and attempts to warn people about forthcoming events.

140   **The way people around San Juan Capistrano:** Named the Juaneño by the Spanish after Mission San Juan Capistrano, which was established near their village of Puttidum, their territory extended approximately from Aliso Creek in Orange County in the north to San Onofre in the south, inland to the Santa Ana mountains. The people now call themselves the Acjachemen.

140   **People from around Los Angeles:** Named the Gabrielino by the Spanish after Mission San Gabriel Arcángel, the Tongva occupied the area from approximately Topanga Canyon in the northwest, through the San Fernando Valley to San Bernadino in the east, and south to Orange County's Aliso Creek. The Tongva also occupied the southern Channel Islands (Catalina, San Clemente, and San Nicolas). The Tongva are part of the Uto-Aztecan language family, one of the largest in the Americas, which includes, among others, the Aztec, Comanche, Hopi, and Paiute. The Takic branch of this family includes all the languages and dialects spoken in Southern California except the Chumash. The main Takic-speaking tribes are the Tongva, the Quechnajuichom (Luiseños), Acjachemen (Juaneños), Cahuillas, Cupeños, Serranos, Tatavium, and Kitanemuk. The contemporary place names of Cucamunga, Tujunga, Topanga, and Cahuenga, among others, are derived from Tongva village names ("nga" translates to "place of").

The Tongva myth was recorded in both Father Gerónimo Boscana's *Chinigchinich* and the anno

People from around Los Angeles (*cont.*)
tations John Peabody Harrington later wrote
for the book. *Chinigchinich* is a collection of Boscana's observations of indigenous culture made
while he served at Mission San Juan Capistrano
from 1814 to 1826. Combined with Harrington's
thorough annotations, Boscana's book is considered to be the most important early source of
information about Native American life in Southern California.

John Harrington (1884–1961), a linguist and ec-
centric genius, devoted his life to recording indigenous languages and cultures, especially in
Southern California. Most of his work was never published since he spent his days and nights
discovering and collecting, leaving a plethora of
scrawled notes stashed, along with food wrap-
pers and other odd bits. In her memoir, *Encounter
with an Angry God*, Harrington's ex-wife, Carobeth Laird, describes working with him as they
traveled the dirt roads of Southern California in
a Model T Ford. Her subsequent marriage to her
Chemehuevi informant, George Laird, unfolds as
a moving love story.

140 **Others who live around Ventura:** This refers
to the southern Chumash, named Ventureño by
the Spanish after Mission San Buenaventura. The
Chumash live in the territory between San Luis
Obispo and Malibu, inland to the western edge
of the San Joaquin Valley and westward to the
northern Channel Islands (Santa Cruz, Anacapa,
Santa Rosa, and San Miguel). The names of
Malibu, Lompoc, Ojai, Pismo Beach, Point
Mugu, Piru, Lake Castaic, and Simi Valley,
among others, are derived from Chumash words.
The Chumash language, once believed to be part
of the Hokan language family, is now thought to
be a unique family with about six dialects.

According to King, Chumash deities behaved
independently of human desires. Astrologers
could observe their behavior and use this information to make predictions, but prayer had little
effect on the Sun, the North Star, Venus, Swordfish, or other major entities. Since the Takic gods
were once people, they continued to be inter-
ested in people's affairs. They were prayed to
and were believed to punish and reward people.
King told me, "I associate the difference between
Chumash and Takic religions to the greater im-
portance of economic control among the Chumash and political control among the Takic peo-

ple. The Chumash are more apt to believe that
something happens because of profit motives
while Takic people attribute events to the will
of the gods. There are few examples of gods af-
fecting people in Blackburn's *December's Child* [a
collection of Chumash myths] except as a con-
sequence of their normal behavior; for example, the sun and swordfish eating people and the
north star providing bounty. Takic religions were
more theistic than Chumash religions."

141 **Still other people who live near the coast:** This
refers especially to the Acjachemen (Juañeno)
and the Tongva (Gabrielino). Within tribes there
are differences in mythology and culture
between the people who live in the interior
and those who live near the coast. This version
comes from Boscana and Harrington's
annotations.

142 **Still there is no light:** This myth was told to Du-
Bois by Cuevish.

142 **Hainit Yunenkit:** This myth was told to DuBois
by Cuevish. Sacred words are paired in Quechnajuichom (Luiseño) myths. In *Aboriginal Society in Southern California* William Duncan Strong
suggests that the doubling gives a general and
then a specific description. DuBois speculates
that each word in the pair serves to extend and
refine the meaning of the other. This practice
brings to mind the Old English manner of cre-
ating names from compounded words, such as
the name Hrothgar in *Beowulf* which was created
from words meaning "glory" and "spear" (as observed by Seamus Heaney in the introduction to
his translation).

144 *Gazing across:* "A Song of Temecula," about the
First People who emerged at Temecula, was
sung for Helen Hunt Roberts by Flora Pa'henim,
a Quechnajuichom (Luiseño). Songs belonging
to the family of a myth teller are interspersed in
the recitation of the myths. Roberts continued
DuBois's work recording ceremonial songs. Her
book, *Form in Primitive Music*, includes translations of the songs she recorded. Unfortunately,
most of the songs DuBois recorded have not yet
been translated. The songs included here are my
versions of the translated songs. In a personal
note to Roberts, Harrington described the typi-
cal, elaborate performance of Quechnajuichom
(Luiseño) songs. (See Harrington's notes at reel
121, frame 0286–0291.)

146 *The sun:* This song was sung to DuBois by
Cuevish.

2. The Great Captain Wiyot: Death, Spirit, Power

151 *ayelkwi:* Southern California shamanism can be understood as the study and acquisition of *ayelkwi,* or knowledge-power. For an in-depth discussion see Raymond White's article, "Luiseño Social Organization," and Lowell Bean's *California Indian Shamanism.* Pragmatic and objective, the shamanistic worldview is based not so much on belief as it is on verifiable and effective outcomes as deduced from repeated observation and experimentation.

151 **One day:** This is based on Cuevas's version as told to DuBois.

152 *Now the spider web:* "Song of the Daylight," a seasonal song about April, is sung by Cuevas and recorded by DuBois.

152 **The way some people:** This is from the Quechnajuichom (Luiseño) creation myth as recorded by Boscana.

152 **Wiyot called together his People:** This is Cuevish's version as told to DuBois.

154 **The calendar unfolded:** Harrington, in his notes on Boscana, summarizes and clarifies the Acjachemen (Juaneño) calendar that DuBois recorded. According to Harrington, calendars are based on the moon and recorded in songs, which also maintain the balance and cycle of the year.

155 **Now he spoke:** This passage is from Harrington's annotations on Boscana.

156 **Another way:** Povunga is a Tongva village, a portion of which is located on what is now the campus of California State University, Long Beach.

156 **Doctors of the people-to-come:** In "The Luiseño Theory of Knowledge," Raymond White describes how doctors viewed the Spanish and Mexican cultures as sources of new forms of *ayelkwi* (knowledge-power), especially ways of curing the new diseases.

159 *Coyote, Coyote:* "A Song Belonging to Andrés Tortuga" was recorded by Helen Hunt Roberts. It originally belonged to the father of her Quechnajuichom (Luiseño) interpreter, Jim Tortuga. Roberts speculates that it is part of a class of songs about Coyote eating Wiyot's heart.

161 *Wiyot's white ashes:* "Tcutcemic 'Fiesta Song'" was sung by Celestino Awaíu, Quechnajuichom (Luiseño), for Helen Hunt Roberts. The word "fiesta" here indicates a ceremony.

163 *Beneath the sacred milkweed string:* This song was recorded in 1903 by C. Hart Merriam and published in his *Studies of California Indians.* He describes it as being sung as part of the conclusion of a Tongva mourning ceremony when the son of a captain, dressed in ritual regalia and body paint, "dances violently on the spot where the [cremation] fire was, whirling rapidly and irregularly, while the singers, surrounding him in a circle, addressed the dead singing" (84).

164 *When it was time to die:* This is a Kwinamish or spirit song sung for DuBois by Jose Albañas, one of her Quechnajuichom (Luiseño) informants.

164 **As Eagle grew sick:** Throughout Southern California, Eagle is one of the most significant First People. According to Harrington's linguistic analysis, the heart is where the spirit of the individual resides; it is the center of each person. This suggests the significance of Coyote's eating Wiyot's heart, which brought death into the world. (Also, eating is a way to take on another being's *ayelkwi.*) The breath, however, is associated with the Milky Way (where the spirit goes after death), suggesting that it is the breath that moves on to the next world.

Alfred Kroeber, on the other hand, identifies the heart as the spirit that flies to the Milky Way and breath as the spirit that goes to the Tomul, the Above and Below of this world. Though not universally accepted, Harrington asserts that only the spirits of captains and doctors go to the Milky Way after death, while the spirits of all others journey to an afterlife in the Above and Below.

164 **Some people around San Pedro:** This is a Tongva (Gabrielino) belief that was recorded by Boscana and discussed by Harrington in his annotations.

164 *In the morning:* "A Song for the Morning after the Night of Watching" was sung for Roberts by Celestino Awaíu, Quechnajuichom (Luiseño).

165 *My heart goes crying:* "Luiseño Song about the Death of a Person" was sung for Roberts by Celestino Awaíu, Quechnajuichom (Luiseño).

3. Food, Feasting, Deer, Moon

169 **The People told him:** As told to DuBois by Cuevish and Cuevas.

171 **Spirits who see us:** "Song for Killing Deer" was sung to Roberts by Celestino Awaíu, Quechnajuichom (Luiseño), who told her that it was sung before a hunt.

171 *I walk and sing:* The following ceremonial songs—"First Song of the Deer Hunting Cycle," "Second Song of the Deer Hunting Cycle," "Third Song of the Deer Hunting Cycle"—were sung to Roberts by Celestino Awaíu, Quechnajuichom (Luiseño). Roberts notes that the songs probably belong to both the Tongva (Gabrielino) and Quechnajuichom (Luiseño). Based on the myth that tells how the First People chose their food after the death of Wiyot, the songs may also have been sung during the Ant Ordeal of the girl's initiation ceremony.

174 *Noise echoed:* "Nokwa'nic Song" was sung to Roberts by Celestino Awaíu, Quechnajuichom (Luiseño). *Nokwanish*, as DuBois spelled it, are songs sung in memory of the dead.

4. The First People

179 **Among them are:** The star lore comes from Quechnajuichom (Luiseño) myths recorded by DuBois and Harrington's annotations on Boscana.

181 **In the Simi Hills:** Huwam is the Chumash name for the village located in the borderland between the Chumash and the Tongva (Gabrielino), who called it 'Atavsanga.

181 **The people around Ventura and Calabasas:** These are the southern Chumash and the Tongva (Gabrielino). *Tswaya tsuqele* is a Chumash word that, according to archaeologist John Romani, describes the Chumash practice of placing feathered poles to mark mountain shrines, especially during the ceremonial season of the Winter Solstice.

181 **Kas'élewun:** A Chumash word that King and others speculate is the origin of the name Castle Peak.

183 **After Wiyot died:** This resumes the Quechnajuichom (Luiseño) myths recorded by DuBois.

183 **They drew the first ground painting:** According to DuBois, ground paintings (sandpaintings) created by many Southern California tribes were used in *toloache* (datura) rituals and by doctors to heal or cause sickness and to create earthquakes.
  Representing the three-part division of the universe, the paintings were spiritual, astrological, and geographical maps that included symbols of animals, insects, and humans. The power in the painting was activated at the end of the ceremony, just before it was destroyed, when one of the participants spat into the hole in the center. Bill Cohen's article, "Indian Sandpaintings of Southern California," is an in-depth source of information on this subject.

184 **Sometimes doctors:** Kroeber, in his *Handbook of the Indians of California*, describes a similar ritual in his discussion of the Tongva, who believe that two gigantic snakes coil at the base of the world and can hear the doctors singing. Cohen suggests that the cords might symbolize the snakes, whose movement causes the earth to quake.

184 **It was Eagle:** This Quechnajuichom (Luiseño) myth was recorded by DuBois.

186 **The four-holed flute:** Harrington lists these instruments, used throughout Southern California, in his notes on Boscana.

187 **People from Ventura:** This refers to the Chumash.

188 *The words of my song:* This gambling song is transcribed in Harrington's field notes (reel 105, frame 0456). After the arrival of the Spanish the game came to be called Peón, referring to the marked pieces of bone that are used like dice. More than a game, gambling expresses personal and group knowledge-power.

188 **The Ventura people say that Sun:** According to Thomas Blackburn in *December's Child*, the Chumash don't have a creation myth like the Tongva (Gabrielino), Acjachemen (Juaneño), Quechnajuichom (Luiseño), and the other Takic-speaking tribes. They assume that the universe, with its three, or in some versions five, layers has always been here. Human beings occupy the middle region, which rests upon two gigantic snakes. Chronological time is unimportant, though the past is divided into two sections: the universal flood that caused the First People to become the natural world and, thereafter, the creation of human beings, the arrival of the Europeans, and the devastating consequences that followed. Blackburn outlines a complex and sophisticated worldview that considers all things to be, in varying measure, alive, intelligent, dangerous, and sacred.

190 **Around Tejon:** This is taken from a ritual speech recorded by Harrington in his notes about the Kitanamuck, the people of the western Antelope Valley and Tehachapi Mountains, and cited in Travis Hudson and Ernest Underhay's *Crystals in the Sky*.

190 **During the Winter Solstice ceremonies:** This refers to the Chumash. See Hudson and Underhay for a detailed description of winter solstice ceremonies and shrines.

193 **In the Simi Hills:** In *December's Children* Blackburn includes the myth (story #30), which may be the basis for the central imagery of the winter solstice petroglyph at Burro Flats in the Simi Hills along the Chumash-Tongva border. (I think of this shrine as the Stonehenge of Southern California.) Bob Edberg's essay, "Shamans and Chiefs," examines the painting and its ritual significance. Chester King is investigating the possibility that it may also have been used as part of a fall equinox ritual. The Burro Flats area has many shrines and glyphs, including a summer solstice ritual site where a notched sandstone peak casts a shadow that moves across a carved bear paw and a rock lined with cupules. John and Gwen Romani and Dan Larson, in "Archaeoastronomical Investigations at Burro Flats," discuss this site in detail.

193 **When Wiyot died:** In his notes on Boscana, Harrington describes the frightening Takwish and recounts this remarkable battle between two seriously powerful First People. Though this account is recorded from Tongva (Gabrielino) and Acjachemen (Juaneño) sources, people throughout the region know about Takwish. According to Harrington, Raven's name, Tukuupar, is the Tongva word for sky, and in "The Culture of the Luiseño Indians," Philip Stedman Sparkman notes that Raven's arrows are made of crystals.

198 **to cure the large and small scalps:** Strong, among others, writes that the Quechnajuichom (Luiseño) and Southern California cultures generally identify human hair with power and with the spirit world, especially the human spirit that leaves the body after death, and with the spirit home of the Milky Way. Hair plays a role in many Southern California myths, and ceremonial ropes, headbands, and bracelets are woven from human hair.

201 **Some people are homosexual:** Boscana disapprovingly observed the presence of homosexuals among the Acjachemen (Juaneño), while Harrington, in his annotations, observes that the practice was accepted as a natural part of human society. According to McCawley it was also part of Tongva (Gabrielino) culture. More information on sexual diversity in Native American cultures is available in Walter Williams's *The Spirit and the Flesh.*

201 **The way they say it around Palm Springs:** In 1925, through interpreter Julian Nortes, Strong recorded Alejo Potencio's version of the Cahuilla creation myth that includes the myth of Moon Young Woman. Strong worked with Southern California people, especially the Cahuillas, Quechnajuichom (Luiseño), and Cupeño, in the mid-1920s. The sexual transgression in this myth, as in the Quechnajuichom (Luiseño) creation myth narrated by Lucario Cuevish, is never stated directly. Strong explains: "They don't make clear what happened for that was a great sin of the creator" (138). The problem of rape and incest in these myths is reminiscent of the same acts in the Mesoamerican myth of Quetzalcoatl.

204 **Feuds between families:** The practice of song wars was documented by Harrington and by Hugo Reid, a Scotsman who emigrated to Los Angeles in 1832 and married a Tongva (Gabrielino) woman named Victoria. Reid wrote a series of letters about the Tongva, containing information he learned from his wife, which were published serially in 1852 in the *Los Angeles Star* newspaper. They were later collected in a book, *The Indians of Los Angeles County.*

205 **She told them:** This part of the Moon Young Woman myth establishes moieties, a totemic social and ancestral structure described by Bean in the introduction to this book.

205 *The ground for my new house:* This marriage song is recounted in Harrington's notes on Boscana.

206 **One day, the ocean:** This Quechnajuichom (Luiseño) version of the flood myth was recorded by DuBois and also by Harrington in his field notes (reel 121, frame 0428).

206 **On top of Katukto:** Harrington, in his Boscana notes, identifies Katukto as both Morro Hill inland from Oceanside and Red Hill near Irvine.

206 **The way people in Ventura:** This refers to the Chumash. Blackburn includes stories about the flood in *December's Child.*

207 **After the water receded:** This continues the Quechnajuichom (Luiseño) myth drawn from DuBois and Harrington's notes on Boscana. Harrington locates Kalaupa as Saddleback Mountain formed by Modjeska and Santiago Peaks.

5. Human Beings: Singers, Balance Keepers

211 **The migrating groups of First People:** This Quechnajuichom (Luiseño) myth was recorded by DuBois.

213 **the First People gathered:** Povunga, one of the most important sacred sites in Southern California, continues to serve as a ritual site for ceremonies and community gatherings. Efforts to preserve it from development are ongoing.

214 **Around Palm Springs:** This version of the Cahuilla creation myth was told to Strong by Potencio, a ceremonial captain. Though he transcribed the myth as prose, Strong reports that every line was sung, with each line forming a verse that is usually repeated. Strong also notes that "the song takes three nights to sing completely. It varies slightly from group to group, and the variations of any two widely separated Cahuilla groups are different in detail though the general motifs are the same" (130).

219 **Some people say that the fly:** This information is from Hansjakob Seiler's bilingual transcription of Joe Lomas's recitation of the Cahuilla creation myth.

220 **Around Ventura and Santa Barbara:** The following are Chumash myths found in Blackburn's *December's Child.*

220 **After the great flood:** Another myth concerning the creation of human beings was recorded by Harrington in his field notes between 1917 and 1918 from Kitanamuck and Chumash people living at Tejon Ranch. Hudson and Blackburn include it in their essay "The Northern Complex." The following is my version:

224 **Some old people:** Blackburn includes this description in *December's Children,* p. 97.

The way people around the Antelope Valley say it, the human beings were created this way:
Almost all the First People drowned or turned into animals
when the great flood
    covered the whole world, even the highest peaks.

Five brothers and their sister, Tsuqqit, were the only ones who survived.
They stayed safely in their beautiful homeland to the south
    where the weather is never hot
        and the land is always carpeted with flowers.

Though the brothers lived separately from their sister,
    one of them, Hukaht, Deer,
            began secretly visiting Tsuqqit at night.
She became pregnant and gave birth to Hummingbird.
As punishment for what he had done,
    Hukaht lost his arm and leg bones,
            so he could never again move around.

Tsuqqit had many children
        who are the ancestors of the people today,
                the human beings.

Since she was the wisest of all, she taught people how to behave
        and all the skills they needed to live here.
She taught them were how to hunt and make tools,
        how to weave baskets and prepare the tobacco,
        how to create the sacred enclosure, and many other skills.

When she finished these instructions,
                    she told them whom to marry,
                         where to live,
                              which languages to speak,
                    and then sent them away to their new homes.

Tsuqqit created everyone except Coyote.

One day, after Tsuqqit finished her usual task of brushing her hair
                    and tossing away the debris,
                              Coyote appeared on the spot where it landed.
     Her oldest brother questioned each of his younger brothers, asking,
          "How can you say there are no other people than ourselves,
                                   when there is Coyote?"

Only one brother, Papamas, "Clouds Running Before the Wind,"
     was able to explain it.
          "We are the only ones," he said.
          "What you see is no person.
                    What you see is Coyote."

Tsuqqit and her brothers still live in their cool and flowered homeland.
     The new people face south when they sing to them, seeking their care.

225 **Oyaison was captain:** Boscana devotes a chapter to the mythic founding of the Acjachemen (Juaneño) village Puttidum, where Mission San Juan Capistrano was founded. Harrington annotates this chapter extensively. In 2002 a coalition of Acjachemen (Juaneño) groups and their supporters worked tirelessly to save the last remnant of land that preserved the village site, but it was bulldozed and covered over by a Catholic high school.

226 **Because power:** This concept is reminiscent of the principle of entropy. The subsequent passages, which reflect the fundamental worldview held by the people of Southern California, are from analyses in Bean's *Mukat's People* and Blackburn's *December's Child*.

228 **Rawi'jawi:** An extraordinary, tragic myth evocative of Greek myths, this was recorded by Carobeth Laird while she was working with and married to Harrington. In a personal letter to Bob Edberg and in her field notes, she describes sitting around the kitchen table after dinner with Juan Menéndez, whose mother was Chumash and Tongva, and Juan's Tongva wife, Juana, at their home in Calabasas, now called the Leonis Adobe. As he spoke he walked his fingers around the table to illustrate Rawi'jawi's journey. Laird advises pronouncing the r sound like a growled "khr." The glottal stop is indicated by the apostrophe. Chester King, in *Overview of the History of American Indians in the Santa Monica Mountains*, suggests that the Rawi'jawi myth lays out a ritual geography of political relationships, social values, and cosmology. He argues that it is the most important extant Tongva (Gabrielino) myth, and believes that it may have been sung as part of mourning ceremonies. He also notes how Castle Peak and the Cave of Munits, central locations in the myth, represent the three layers of the cosmos: Above (the peak), Below (inside the cave), and Middle (the world between). Reid included a shorter version of the myth in his letters that is less geographically specific than the Menéndez version.

233 **Munits was a cannibal:** Munits's cave is known today as Bat Cave. In 2003, after a decades-long battle, the Ahmanson Ranch, which included land adjacent to the cave that was slated to be a golf course, was saved from development and sold to the state. Owls still live in the cave and datura grows near its mouth.

6. White People

243 **The people around Palm Springs:** Strong's record of Alejo Patencio's recitation of the Cahuilla creation myth includes this myth. Francisco Patencio's *Stories and Legends of the Palm Springs Indians* and Lucille Hooper's "The Cahuilla Indians" also include the origins of White People.

Epilogue. Chinigchinich, the Spanish, the Yankees

247 **Life expectancy:** This is the figure for San Gabriel Mission according to McCawley.

247 **Many ages:** Many scholars believe that the myth of Chinigchinich probably emerged on the Channel Islands as a revision of earlier myths, after the first contact with the Spanish. However, King believes that it is more likely a precontact myth and not an effort at revitalism. In his view Chinigchinich is similar to the Aztec feathered serpent and was probably a Chumash *'antap* dancer with knowledge of the sacred. King views Chinigchinich as a mythic founder and culture hero of Tongva (Gabrielino) society.

248 **He appeared:** Harrington's annotations on Boscana's *Chinigchinich* and his field notes provide a detailed portrait of the myth, its rituals, and associated stories. DuBois's record of the religion of the Quechnajuichom (Luiseño) is another important source of information about the Chinigchinich myth. Bean and Vane's chapter in the *Handbook of North American Indians* describes the use of datura in the Chinigchinich ceremonies.

249 **They still dance:** Doctors throughout the region led fire dances. Strong describes a Cahuilla Fire Dance that closed the *toloache* (datura) ritual of the boys' initiation: "A large fire was built outside of the dance house. Both men and women of the clan surrounded it and moved around the fire singing and dancing, sometimes at a fast, sometimes at a slow pace. Then after the dance had become fast and there was much excitement all the men sat down around the fire and pushed it in with their feet. Men did not burn, informants say, but they often became unconscious from the heat, the shamans fanning them with feathers to bring them to. Then all the men changed position and used their hands in putting out the fire. The shamans occasionally jumped into the fire and kicked the coals around with their bare feet, but they likewise did not burn. The women and children stood outside the circle and looked on,

chanting the songs for this particular ceremony, which are about ten in number. Finally, the fire was entirely extinguished and the ceremony ended" (176–77).

253 **Feather skirt:** Throughout Southern California the condor is one of the most important First People and plays a role in mourning and other rituals (similar to the eagle).

254 **Do you see this:** Sparkman, who is quoted in Kroeber's *Handbook of the Indians of California*, records lengthy versions of the Quechnajuichom (Luiseño) boys' and girls' initiation lectures. In his commentary Kroeber observes that these speeches suggest a culture based on "manners rather than morals" and that focuses on the "innumerable but little relations of daily life." He notes that the language doesn't contain terms for right and wrong. Rather, "affability, liberality, restraint of anger and jealousy, politeness" are highly valued and encouraged. "Virtue," he writes, "is far from being its own reward—it is the only path that leads to prosperity" (683).

257 **1775:** The history of revolts by indigenous people against the Spanish can be found in McCawley and in the work of Maria Lepowsky and Steven Hackel. White observes that, at the time of the Spanish arrival, the Quechnajuichom (Luiseño) were deeply involved in inter-village warfare because they were "preoccupied with internecine *ayelkwi* struggles." As a result, they didn't revolt and were easily conquered.

258 **1823:** Harrington, in his Boscana annotations, discusses the indigenous response to the appearance of comets over Southern California.

258 **1824:** This account comes from Lepowsky's lecture, "Dances and Pagan Abuses," quoting Harrington's Chumash field notes, especially his interview of Maria Solaris.

260 **1917:** Laird's handwritten record of this story, told by Juan Menéndez about his Tongva mother-in-law who had converted at San Gabriel Mission, and a friend, Estevan, is included in Harrington's field notes (reel 106, frame 0215).

Apodaca, Paul. "Tradition, Myth, and Performance of Cahuilla Bird Songs." PhD diss., University of California, Los Angeles, 1999.

Applegate, Richard B. *Atishwin: The Dream Helper in South-Central California*. Ballena Press Anthropological Papers 13, edited by L. J. Bean and T. C. Blackburn. Socorro NM: Ballena Press, 1978.

Atwater, T. "Plate Tectonic History of Southern California with Emphasis on the Western Transverse Ranges and Santa Rosa Island." In *Contributions to the Geology of the Northern Channel Islands*, edited by P. W. Weigand, 1–8. American Association of Petroleum Geologists, Pacific Section, MP 45 (1998).

———. "San Andreas: An Animated Tectonic History of Western North America and Southern California." Educational Multimedia Visualization Center, University of California Santa Barbara. http://emvc.geol.ucsb.edu/downloads.php#RegionalTectGeolHist

Austin, Paige. "Workers Ordered Off Tribal Graves." *Orange County Register*, October 1, 2002, A1.

Axelrod, Daniel I. *Mio-Pliocene Floras from West-Central Nevada*. University of California Publications in Geological Sciences 33, edited by W. C. Putnam, C. Durrell, and G. Tunell. Berkeley CA: University of California Press, 1956.

Bakker, Elna S. *An Island Called California: An Ecological Introduction to its Natural Communities*. 2nd ed. Berkeley CA: University of California Press, 1984.

Ball, Phillip. *Life's Matrix: A Biography of Water*. Berkeley CA: University of California Press, 2001.

Barnes, Lawrence G. Interview by author. Los Angeles CA, March 1998.

Barnes, Lawrence G., and Samuel A. McLeod. "The Fossil Record and Phyletic Relationships of Gray Whales." In *The Gray Whale*, edited by M. L. Jones, S. L. Swartz, and S. Leatherwood. London: Academic Press, 1984.

Barth, Andrew P., J. Lawford Anderson, Carl E. Jacobson, Scott R. Paterson, and Joseph L. Wooden.

"Magmatism and Tectonics in a Tilted Crustal Section through a Continental Arc, Eastern Transverse Ranges and Southern Mojave Desert." In *Field Guide to Plutons, Volcanoes, Faults, Reefs, Dinosaurs, and Possible Glaciation in Selected Areas of Arizona, California, and Nevada*, edited by Ernest M. Duebendorfer and Eugene I. Smith, 101–17. The Geological Society of America, Field Guide 11, 2008.

Bean, Lowell John. *Mukat's People: The Cahuilla Indians of Southern California*. Berkeley CA: University of California Press, 1972.

———. "Cahuilla." In *Handbook of North American Indians, Vol. 8: California*, edited by Robert F. Heizer, 575–87. Washington DC: Smithsonian Institution, 1978.

———. "Power and Its Applications in Native California." In *Native Californians: A Theoretical Perspective*, edited by Lowell John Bean and Thomas C. Blackburn, 99–123. Menlo Park CA: Ballena Press, 1976.

———. "Social Organization in Native California." In *Native Californians: A Theoretical Perspective*, edited by Lowell John Bean and Thomas C. Blackburn, 99–123. Menlo Park CA: Ballena Press, 1976.

———. "Indians of Southern California." *Anthropology of the Americas Masterkey* 59, no. 2 (1985): 32–41.

———. ed. *California Indian Shamanism*. Ballena Press Anthropological Papers 39. Menlo Park CA: Ballena Press, 1992.

Bean, Lowell John, and Charles R. Smith. "Gabrielino." In *Handbook of North American Indians, Vol. 8: California*, edited by Robert F. Heizer, 538–49. Washington DC: Smithsonian Institution, 1978.

———. "Cupeño." In *Handbook of North American Indians, Vol. 8: California*, edited by Robert F. Heizer, 588–91. Washington DC: Smithsonian Institution, 1978.

———. "Serrano." In *Handbook of North American Indians, Vol. 8: California*, edited by Robert F. Heizer, 570–74. Washington DC: Smithsonian Institution, 1978.

Bean, Lowell John, and Florence C. Shipek. "Luiseño." In *Handbook of North American Indians, Vol. 8: California*, edited by Robert F. Heizer, 550–63. Washington DC: Smithsonian Institution, 1978.

Bean, Lowell John, and Sylvia Brakke Vane. "Cults and Their Transformations." In *Handbook of North American Indians, Vol. 8: California*, edited by Robert F. Heizer, 662–72. Washington DC: Smithsonian Institution, 1978.

Beebe, Rose Marie, and Robert M. Senkewicz. *Lands of Promise and Despair: Chronicles of Early California, 1535–1846*. Santa Clara CA: Santa Clara University: Heyday Books, 2001.

Bell, Horace. *Leonis or The Lion's Brood*. Edited by G. K. Hoppe. Calabasas CA: Leonis Adobe Association, 1993.

Benedict, Ruth. "Serrano Tales." *The Journal of American Folklore* 39, no. 151 (January–March, 1926): 1–17.

Benson, Arlene, and Tom Hoskinson, eds. *Earth and Sky: Papers from the Northridge Conference on Aarchaeoastronomy*. Thousand Oaks CA: Slo'w Press, 1985.

Bierhorst, John. *The Way of the Earth: Native America and the Environment*. New York: William Morrow, 1994.

Bigger, Richard. *Flood Control in Metropolitan Los Angeles*. University of California Publications in Political Science 6, edited by D. G. Farrelly, J. C. Coleman, and D. Marvick. Berkeley CA: University of California Press, 1959.

Blackburn, Thomas C. *Ethnohistoric Descriptions of Gabrielino Material Culture*. Annual Report: Archaeological Survey. Los Angeles, 1963.

———, ed. *Flowers of the Wind: Papers on Ritual, Myth, and Symbolism in California and the Southwest*. Socorro NM: Ballena Press, 1977.

———, ed. *December's Child: A Book of Chumash Oral Narratives, Collected by J. P. Harrington*. Berkeley CA: University of California Press, 1975.

Blackburn, Thomas C., and Lowell John Bean. "Kitanemuck." In *Handbook of North American Indians, Vol. 8: California*, edited by Robert F. Heizer, 564–69. Washington DC: Smithsonian Institution, 1978.

Blair, James. "Upside of El Nino's Thrashing: Fossil Finds Galore." *Christian Science Monitor*, June 22, 1998.

Boscana, Father Gerónimo. *Chinigchinich: A Revised and Annotated Version of Alfred Robinson's Translation of Father Gerónimo Boscana's Historical Account of the Belief, Usages, Customs and Extravagancies of the Indians of this Mission of San Juan Capistrano Called the Acagchemem Tribe*. Santa Ana CA: Fine Arts Press, 1933; reprint, Banning CA: Malki Museum Press, 1978.

Bower, Bruce. "African Legacy: Fossils Plug Gap in Human Origins." *Science News*, June 14, 2003, 371.

———. "Lucy's Kind Takes Humanlike Turn." *Science News*, July 19, 2003, 45.

Bright, William. Preface. In Father Gerónimo Boscana, *Chinigchinich: A Revised and Annotated Version of Alfred Robinson's Translation of Father Gerónimo Boscana's Historical Account of the Belief, Usages, Customs and Extravagancies of the Indians of this Mission of San Juan Capistrano Called the Acagchemem Tribe*. Santa Ana CA: Fine Arts Press, 1933; reprint, Banning CA: Malki Museum Press, 1978.

Bridge, Kay. "My Uncle Went to the Moon." *Artscanada* (December 1973–January 1974): 154–58.

Bryan, Bruce. *Archaeological Explorations on San Nicolas Island*. Southwest Museum Papers 22. Highland Park CA: Southwest Museum, 1970.

Bussino, Giovanni R., and Lawrence G. Barnes. "The Lincoln Heights Whale." *Terra* 22, no. 4 (Natural History Museum of Los Angeles County) (March–April, 1984): 16–19.

California Department of Parks and Recreation. *Rock Art of Malibu Creek State Park: LAn-748*, ed. William D. Hyder and Kathleen Conti. Santa Barbara CA, 1990.

California Department of Water Resources. *Mineral and Water Resources of California, Part II*. Committee Print ed. Washington DC: U.S. Government Printing Office, 1966.

Campbell, Paul. *Survival Skills of Native California*. Salt Lake City UT: Gibbs Smith, 1999.

Campbell, Russell, and R. F. Yerkes. *Geologic Guide to the Stratigraphy and Structure of the Topanga Group, Central Santa Monica Mountains, Southern California*. Los Angeles Basin Geological Society Guidebook 49. Bakersfield CA: Los Angeles Basin Geological Society, 1980.

Carrico, Richard L. "Sociopolitical Aspects of the 1775 Revolt at Mission San Diego de Alcala: an Ethnohistorical Approach." *The Journal of San Diego History* 43, no. 3 (Summer 1997). http://sandiegohistory.org/journal/97summer/missionrevolt.htm

Castillo, Edward D. "The Impact of Euro-American Exploration and Settlement." In *Handbook of North American Indians, Vol. 8: California*, edited by Robert F. Heizer, 99–127. Washington DC: Smithsonian Institution, 1978.

Cattermole, Peter. *Building Planet Earth*. Cambridge:

Cambridge University Press, 2000.

Chandler, Mark A. "The Climate of the Pliocene: Simulating Earth's Last Great Warm Period." Goddard Institute for Space Studies (April 1997). http://www.giss.nasa.gov/research/features/pliocene/.

Chang, Kenneth. "Diamonds Linked to Quick Cooling Eons Ago." *New York Times*, January 2, 2009, A13.

Chittenden, Russell H. *Biographical Memoir of William Henry Brewer, 1828–1910*. National Academy of Sciences Biographical Memoirs 12, no. 9 (1927).

Chong, Jai-Rui. "Wildfires Lead to Peek at Serrano Indian History." *Los Angeles Times*, December 6, 2003, B1.

Cline, David B. "The Search for Dark Matter." In "Majestic Universe," special issue of *Scientific American* (2004): 56–63.

Clottes, Jean, and David Lewis-Williams. *The Shamans of Prehistory: Trance and Magic in the Painted Caves*. Translated by S. Hawkes. New York: Henry N. Abrams, 1996.

Cohen, Bill. "Indian Sandpaintings of Southern California." *Journal of California and Great Basin Anthropology* 9, no. 1 (1987): 4–34.

Cohen, Chester G. *El Escorpion*. Woodland Hills CA: Periday, 1989.

Cole, K. C. *The Hole in the Universe: How Scientists Peered Over the Edge of Emptiness and Found Everything*. San Diego CA: Harcourt, 2001.

Cook, Sherburne F. *The Conflict Between the California Indian and White Civilization*. Berkeley CA: University of California Press, 1976.

Cowen, Richard. *History of Life*. 3rd ed. Malden MA: Blackwell Science, 2000.

Cowen, Ron. "In the Beginning: Dark Matter Builds Galaxies, Feeds Quasars." *Science News*, January 25, 2003, 51–52.

———. "Supernova Spectacular." *Science News*, July 19, 2003, 40–44.

———. "Wrenching Findings: Homing in on Dark Energy." *Science News*, February 28, 2004, 132.

Dakin, Susanna Bryant. *A Scotch Paisano in Old Los Angeles: Hugo Reid's Life in California 1832–1852, Derived from His Correspondence*. Berkeley CA: University of California Press, 1978.

Dalziel, Ian W. D. "Pacific Margins of Laurentia and East Antarctica–Australia as a Conjugate Rift Pair: Evidence and Implications for an Eocambrian Supercontinent." *Geology* 19 (1991): 598–601.

Davis, Mike. *Ecology of Fear: Los Angeles and the Imagination of Disaster*. New York: Metropolitan, 1998.

Davies, Paul. *The Last Three Minutes: Conjectures about the Ultimate Fate of the Universe*. New York: Basic Books, 1994.

DeCelles, P.G. "Late Jurassic to Eocene Evolution of the Cordilleran Thrust Belt and Foreland Basin System, Western U.S.A." *American Journal of Science* 304 (February, 2004): 105–68.

de Duve, Christian. *Vital Dust: Life as a Cosmic Imperative*. New York: Basic Books, 1995.

Deverell, William and Greg Hise, eds. *Land of Sunshine: An Environmental History of Metropolotan Los Angeles*. Pittsburgh: University of Pittsburgh Press, 2005.

Dickinson, William R. "Cretaceous Sinistral Strike Slip Along Nacimiento Fault in Coastal California." *The American Association of Petroleum Geologists Bulletin* 67, no. 4 (1983): 624–45.

Dominguez, Susan. "Remembering Lillian." *News from Native California* (Spring 2002): 12–13.

Dott, Jr., Robert H. and Donald R. Prothero. *Evolution of the Earth*. 5th ed. New York: McGraw-Hill, 1994.

Dower, Rick. "Fishing in the Desert." *American Archaeology* 4, no. 4 (Winter 2000–2001): 20–26.

Dozier, Deborah. *The Heart Is Fire: The World of the Cahuilla Indians of Southern California*. Berkeley CA: Heyday, 1998.

DuBois, Constance Goddard. "The Religion of the Luiseño Indians of Southern California." *University of California Publications in American Archaeology and Ethnology* 8, no. 3 (June 27, 1908): 69–186; reprinted New York: Kraus, 1964.

———. "Religious Ceremonies and Myths of the Mission Indians." *American Anthropologist* 7, no. 4 (October–December 1905): 620–29.

———. "Mythology of the Mission Indians." *The Journal of the American Folklore Society* 19, no. 66 (1904): 185–88; no. 72 (1906): 52–60; no. 73 (1906): 145–64.

———. "The Constance Goddard DuBois Papers, 1897–1909." Division of Rare and Manuscript Collections, Cornell University Library Microfilms, Ithaca, New York.

———. "Constance Goddard DuBois Papers and Notes." Division of Anthropology Archives, American Museum of Natural History, New York.

Dunne, George. Interview by author. Northridge CA, July 2002.

Dunne, George, and Jon Sloan. "Owens Valley to the Panamints: Lands of Illusion." Handout at All Department Field Trip to Owens Valley, Northridge CA, May 29–31, 1998.

Dwyer, Gary S. "Unraveling the Signals of Global

Climate Change." *Science*, (January 14, 2000): 246–47.

Edberg, Bob. Letter to author. Santa Monica CA, April 12, 1994.

———. "Shamans and Chiefs: Visions of the Future." In *Earth and Sky: Papers from the Northridge Convergence on Archeoastronomy*, ed. A. Benson and T. Hoskinson. Thousand Oaks CA: Slo'w, 1985.

Eliade, Mircea. *Essential Sacred Writings from around the World*. San Francisco: Harper Collins, 1967.

———. *Shamanism: Archaic Techniques of Ecstasy*. Translated by W. R. Trask. Bollingen Series 76. Princeton: Princeton University Press, 1972.

Elliott, David K. "A Reassessment of *Astraspis desiderata*, the Oldest North American Vertebrate." *Science* 237 (1987): 190–92.

Emery, Kenneth O. "General Geology of the Offshore Area, Southern California." In *Geology of Southern California*, ed. R. H. Jahns. San Francisco: California Department of Natural Resources, Division of Mines, 1954.

Everett, John R., Marie Morisawa, and Nicholas M. Short. "Tectonic Landforms." In *Geomorphology from Space: A Global Overview of Regional Landforms*, ed. Nicholas M. Short Sr. and Robert W. Blair Jr. Washington, DC: NASA, 1986 (OOP). Available online: http://disc.sci.gsfc.nasa.gov/geo morphology/table-of-contents/GEO_2/index .shtml

Fagan, Brian M. *From Black Land to Fifth Sun: The Science of Sacred Sites*. Reading MA: Helix, 1998.

———. *Before California: An Archaeologist Looks at Our Earliest Inhabitants*. Lanhan MA: Rowman & Littlefield, 2003.

Fields, Scott. "Megafloods at Ice Age's End." *Earth: The Science of Our Planet* (May 1994): 12–13.

Finnerty, W. Patrick, Dean A. Decker, Nelson N. Leonard III, Thomas F. King, Chester King, and Linda B. King. "Community Structure and Trade at Isthmus Cove: A Salvage Excavation on Catalina Island." In *Pacific Coast Archaeological Society Occasional Paper* no. 1 (1970): 1–31.

Flannery, Tim. *The Eternal Frontier: An Ecological History of North America and Its Peoples*. New York: Atlantic Monthly, 2001.

Friedman, William E. "Sex among the Flowers." *Natural History* 115, no. 9 (November 2006): 48–53.

Fritsche, A. Eugene. "Preliminary Middle Tertiary Paleogeographic Maps of Area Represented by Two-Degree Los Angeles Map Sheet, California." *American Association of Petroleum Geologists Bulletin* 65 (1981): 927–28.

———. "Miocene Paleogeography of Southwestern California and Its Implications Regarding Basin Terminology." *International Geology Review* 40 (1998): 1–27.

———. Interview by author. Northridge CA, April 16, 1998; and September 12, 2002.

Fritsche, A. Eugene, and Peter W. Weigand, eds. "Geologic History of the Santa Monica Mountains: Rocks, Structures, and Tectonics." Workshop handout, Department of Geological Sciences, Cal. State Northridge, May 19–20, 1995.

Gayton, A. H. "The Orpheus Myth in North America." *The Journal of American Folklore* 48, no. 189 (July–September 1935): 263–93.

Gersonde, R., F. T. Kyte, T. Frederichs, U. Bleil, and G. Kuhn. "New Data on the Late Pliocene Eltanin Impact into the Deep Southern Ocean." Third International Conference on Large Meteorite Impacts, Nordlingen, Germany, Aug. 5–7, 2003.

Glazmaier, Gary A. "Convection in the Core and the Generation of the Earth's Magnetic Field." In *Earth: Inside and Out*, edited by E. A. Mathez. New York: New Press, 2001.

Goebel, Ted, Michael R. Waters, and Dennis H. O'Rourke. "The Late Pleistocene Dispersal of Modern Humans in the Americas." *Science* 319 (March 14, 2008): 1497–502.

Goho, Alexandra. "Clays Catalyze Life?" *Science News*, November 1, 2003.

Gore, Rick. "The Rise of Mammals." *National Geographic* (April 2003): 2–37.

Grant, Campbell. *Rock Art of the American Indian*. New York: Promontory, 1967.

———. *The Rock Paintings of the Chumash*. Santa Barbara CA: Santa Barbara Museum of Natural History, 1993.

———. "Chumash: Introduction." In *Handbook of North American Indians, Vol. 8: California*, edited by Robert F. Heizer, 505–19. Washington DC: Smithsonian Institution, 1978.

Grant, Campbell, James W. Baird, and J. Kenneth Pringle. *Rock Drawings of the Coso Range*. Maturango Museum Publications 4. Ridgecrest CA: Maturango Museum, 1987.

Greene, Brian. *The Elegant Universe: Superstrings, Hidden Dimensions, and the Quest for the Ultimate Theory*. New York: W. W. Norton, 1999.

Gribbin, John. *The Birth of Time: How Astronomers Measured the Age of the Universe*. New Haven CT: Yale Nota Bene, 1999.

Gribbin, John, and Martin Rees. *Cosmic Coincidences:*

Dark Matter, Mankind, and Antrhopic Cosmology. New York: Bantam, 1989.

Gribbin, John, and Mary Gribbin. *Stardust: Supernovae and Life, the Cosmic Connection.* New Haven CT: Yale University Press, 2000.

Groves, Lindsey. Interview by author. Los Angeles, March 26, 1998.

Guinn, J. M. *A History of California and an Extended History of Los Angeles and Environs: Also Containing Biographies of Well-Known Citizens of the Past and Present, Vol.1.* Los Angeles: Historic Record Co., 1915.

Gumprecht, Blake. *The Los Angeles River: Its Life, Death, and Possible Rebirth.* Baltimore: Johns Hopkins University Press, 1999.

Hackel, Steven W. *Children of Coyote, Missionaries of Saint Francis: Indian-Spanish Relations in Colonial California, 1769–1850.* Chapel Hill: University of North Carolina Press, 2005.

———. "Indian Testimony and the Mission San Gabriel Uprising of 1785." *Ethnohistory* 50, no. 4 (Fall 2003): 643–69.

Haldane, David. "Bone Sites Verified at Bolsa Chica Wetlands." *Los Angeles Times*, February 15, 1994, A1.

Harrington, J. P. *John Peabody Harrington Papers, Vol. 3: Southern California/Basin.* Smithsonian Institution, National Anthropological Archives, Washington DC. Microfilm edition, Millwood NY: Kraus International, 1986.

———. "The New Original Version of Boscana's Historical Account of the San Juan Capistrano Indians of Southern California." *Smithsonian Miscellaneous Collections* 92, no. 4 (1934).

———. Annotations. In *Chinigchinich: A Revised and Annotated Version of Alfred Robinson's Translation of Father Gerónimo Boscana's Historical Account of the Belief, Usages, Customs and Extravagancies of the Indians of this Mission of San Juan Capistrano Called the Acagchemem Tribe.* Santa Ana CA: Fine Arts Press, 1933. Reprint, Banning CA: Malki Museum Press, 1978.

Harris, John M., ed. "Rancho La Brea: Death Trap and Treasure Trove." Special issue, *Terra* 38, no. 2 (Natural History Museum of Los Angeles County) (May–June 2001).

Harris, John M., and George T. Jefferson, eds. *Rancho La Brea: Treasures of the Tar Pits.* Los Angeles: Natural History Museum of Los Angeles County, 1985.

Hawking, Stephen W. *A Brief History of Time: From the Big Bang to Black Holes.* New York: Bantam, 1988.

Heaney, Seamus. *Beowulf: A New Verse Translation.* New York: W. W. Norton, 2000.

Hecht, Jeff. "Firebirth: The Moon Was Forged in a Giant Collision that Ripped the Iron From Its Heart." *New Scientist*, August 7, 1999.

Hedges, Ken. "Traversing the Great Gray Middle Ground: An Examination of Shamanistic Interpretation of Rock Art." *American Indian Rock Art* 27 (2001): 123–36.

Heizer, Robert F. "Introduction." In *California*, edited by Robert F. Heizer. *Handbook of North American Indians, Vol. 8.* Washington DC: Smithsonian Institution, 1978, 1–5.

———. Introduction and Notes. In *The Indians of Los Angeles County: Hugo Reid's Letters of 1852*, edited and annotated by Robert F. Heizer: 1–5 Los Angeles, Southwest Museum, 1968.

Heizer, Robert F., and Albert B. Elsasser. *The Natural World of the California Indians.* California Natural History Guides 46. Berkeley CA: University of California Press, 1980.

Heizer, Robert F., and M. A. Whipple, eds. *The California Indians: A Source Book*, 2nd ed. Berkeley CA: University of California Press, 1971.

Hicks, Jack, James D. Houston, Maxine Hong Kingston, and Al Young, eds. *The Literature of California, Vol. 1: Native American Beginnings to 1945.* Berkeley CA: University of California Press, 2000.

Hill, Jane H., and Rosinda Nolasquez, eds. *Mulu'Wetam: The First People, Cupeño Culture, Mythology, and Cupeño Languages Dictionary.* Banning CA: Malki Museum Press, 1973.

Hinds, Norman E. A. *Evolution of the California Landscape.* Department of Natural Resources Bulletin 158. San Francisco: California Department of Natural Resources, 1952.

Hinton, Leanne. *Flutes of Fire: Essays on California Indian Languages.* Berkeley CA: Heyday Books, 1994 (rev. 1996).

Hooper Virtual Natural History Museum. "Speculated Causes for the Cambrian Extinction." *Extinctions: Cycles of Life and Death through Time.* The Department of Earth Sciences, Carleton University, Ottawa, Ontario. http://hoopermuseum.earthsci.carleton.ca//extinction/camcause.html.

Hooper Virtual Natural History Museum. "Mass Extinctions of the Phanerozoic Menu." *Extinctions: Cycles of Life and Death Through Time.* The Department of Earth Sciences, Carleton University, Ottawa, Ontario. http://hoopermuseum.earthsci.carleton.ca//extinction/extincmenu.html.

Hoots, H. W. *Geology of the Eastern Part of the Santa*

Monica Mountains. Washington DC: United States Department of the Interior, 1930.

Hudson, Travis, Thomas Blackburn, Rosario Curletti, and Janice Timbrook. *The Eye of the Flute: Chumash Traditional History and Ritual as told by Fernando Librado Kitsepawit to John P. Harrington.* Santa Barbara CA: Santa Barbara Museum of Natural History, 1977.

Hudson, Travis, and Thomas C. Blackburn. "The Integration of Myth and Ritual and South-Central California: The 'Northern Complex.'" *Journal of California Anthropology* 5, no. 2 (1978): 225–50.

Hudson, Travis, and Ernest Underhay. *Crystals in the Sky: An Intellectual Odyssey Involving Chumash Astronomy, Cosmology, and Rock Art.* Ballena Press Anthropological Papers 10, edited by L. J. Bean and T. C. Blackburn. Menlo Park CA: Ballena, 1978.

Hudson, Travis, Georgia Lee, and Ken Hedges. "Solstice Observers and Observatories in Native California." *Journal of California and Great Basin Anthropology* 1, no. 1 (Summer 1979): 38–63.

Hyde, Villiana Calac, and Eric Elliot. *Yumáyk Yumáyk (Long Ago).* Berkeley CA: University of California Publications in Linguistics 125, 1994.

Ingersoll, Raymond V. "Los Angeles Is on a Voyage Northwest." *Los Angeles Times,* July 1, 1984, D5.

———. "Phanerozoic Tectonic Evolution of Central California and Environs." *International Geology Review* 39 (1997): 957–72.

———. "Tectonostratigraphy of the Santa Monica Mountains, Southern California." Paper read at the 97th Annual Meeting, Pacific Section, American Association of Petroleum Geologists, Universal City CA, April 9–11, 2001.

———. Interview by author. Los Angeles, September 18, 2002.

Ingersoll, Raymond V., and Peter E. Rumelhart. "Three-stage Evolution of the Los Angeles Basin, Southern California." *Geology* 27, no. 7 (1999): 593–96.

Iovin, June. "A Summary Description of Luiseño Material Culture." *Annual Report: Archaeological Survey.* Los Angeles, 1963.

Irwin, William P. "Geology and Plate-Tectonic Development." In *The San Andreas Fault System, California,* edited by Dr. Robert E. Wallace. U.S. Geological Survey Professional Paper 1515. Washington DC: United States Government Printing Office, 1991. Available online: http://www.johnmartin.com/earthquakes/eqsafs/safs_301.htm.

Isozaki, Yukio. "Permo-Triassic Boundary Superanox-ia and Stratified Superocean: Records from Lost Deep Sea." *Science* 276 (April 11, 1997): 235–38.

Jaeger, Edmund, and Arthur C. Smith. *Introduction to the Natural History of Southern California.* Berkeley CA: University of California Press, 1966.

Jurmain, Claudia, and William McCawley. *O, My Ancestor: Recognition and Renewal for the Gabrielino Tongva People of the Los Angeles Area.* Berkeley CA: Heyday, 2009.

Jefferson, George T. Interview by author. Los Angeles, May 29, 1986; September 23, 1992.

Jennings, Francis. *The Founders of America: How Indians Discovered the Land, Pioneered in It, and Created Great Classical Civilizations, How They Were Plunged into a Dark Age by Invasion and Conquest, and How They Are Reviving.* New York: W. W. Norton, 1993.

Johnson, George. "Dark Matters: Afloat in a Cosmic Hall of Mirrors." *New York Times,* March 5, 2000, sec. 4.

Johnson, John. "California: Arlington Springs Remains." *Friends of America's Past.* http://www.friendsofpast.org/earliest-americans/california.html (posted July 31, 2001).

———. "New Area of Exploration Surfaces from the Santa Barbara Channel." *Los Angeles Times,* October 21, 2001, B8.

———. "Ethnohistoric Overview for the Santa Susana Pass State Historic Park Cultural Resources Inventory Project." Prepared for the Southern Service Center, State of California Department of Parks and Recreation. June 2006.

Johnston, Bernice Eastman. *California's Gabrielino Indians.* Los Angeles: Southwest Museum, 1962.

Josephy, A. M., Jr., ed. *America in 1492: The World of the Indian Peoples before the Arrival of Columbus.* New York: Vintage, 1991.

King, Chester. "Early Southern California." In *Encyclopedia of Prehistory Vol. 6: North America,* edited by Peter N. Peregrine and Melvin Ember, 144–57. New York: Kluwer Academic/Plenum, 2001.

———. *Japchibit Ethnohistory.* Prepared for the U.S. Department of Agriculture, Southern California Province. September 29, 2003 (revised November 1, 2003).

———. *Overview of the History of American Indians in the Santa Monica Mountains.* (Draft.) Prepared for the National Park Service Pacific West Region, February 2009.

———. Interview by author. Topanga CA, June 1993; July 2009.

———. "Protohistoric and Historic Archaeology." In

Handbook of North American Indians, Vol. 8: California, edited by Robert F. Heizer, 58–68. Washington DC: Smithsonian Institution, 1978.

King, Chester, and Thomas Blackburn. "Tataviam." In *Handbook of North American Indians, Vol. 8: California*, 535–37. Washington DC: Smithsonian Institution, 1978.

Kious, W. Jacquelyne, and Robert I. Tilling. *This Dynamic Earth: The Story of Plate Tectonics*. Washington DC: U.S. Government Printing Office, 1996. Available online: http://pubs.usgs.gov/gip/dynamic/dynamic.html.

Klesius, Michael. "The Big Bloom." *National Geographic* (July, 2002): 102–121.

Kroeber, A. L. *Handbook of the Indians of California*. New York: Dover, 1976.

———. "The Religion of the Indians of California." *American Archaeology and Ethnology* 4, no. 6 (1907): 319–56.

Krupp, Edward C. *Echoes of the Ancient Skies: The Astronomy of Ancient Civilizations*. New York: Oxford University Press, 1983.

———. "Saluting the Solstice." *News from Native California* 1, no. 5 (November–December 1987): 10–13.

Kuhn, Michael. "Plants and Animals of Simi Valley." In *Simi Valley: A Journey Through Time*, 321–27. Simi Valley CA: Simi Valley Historical Society and Museum, 1997.

Laird, Carobeth. *Encounter with an Angry God: Reflections of My Life with John Peabody Harrington*. Albuquerque NM: University of New Mexico Press, 1975.

———. Letters to Bob Edberg. December 16, 1982; January 27, 1983.

———. *Mirror and Pattern: George Laird's World of Chemehuevi Mythology*. Banning CA: Malki Museum Press, 1984.

Lander, E. Bruce. "Geology and Vertebrate Paleontology of Cenozoic Nonmarine Rock Units in Simi Valley." In *Simi Valley: A Journey Through Time*, 303–319. Simi Valley CA: Simi Valley Historical Society and Museum, 1997.

Laylander, Don. "California's Prehistory as a Remembered Past." *Journal of California and Great Basin Anthropology* 26, no. 2 (2006): 153–77.

Lear, C. H., H. Eiderfield, and P. A. Wilson. "Cenozoic Deep-Sea Temperatures and Global Ice Volumes from Mg/Ca in Benthic Foraminiferal Calcite." *Science* (January 14, 2000): 269–72.

Lepowsky, Maria. "Dances and Pagan Abuses: Ritual Violence and Revitalization Movements in Early Southern California." Lecture, Institute for the Study of the American West, Los Angeles, March 2004.

———. "Indian Revolts and Cargo Cults: Ritual Violence and Revitalization in California and New Guinea." In *Reassessing Revitalization: Perspectives from Native North America and the Pacific Islands*, 1–60, edited by Michael Harkin. Lincoln: University of Nebraska Press, 2004.

Librado, Fernando. *The Eye of the Flute: Chumash Traditional History and Ritual*. 2nd ed. Santa Barbara CA: Santa Barbara Museum of Natural History, 1981.

Liljeblad, Sven. "Oral Tradition: Content and Style of Verbal Arts." *Handbook of North American Indians Vol. 11: Great Basin*. Washington DC: Smithsonian Institution, 1986.

Loomis, William F. *Four Billion Years: An Essay on the Evolution of Genes and Organisms*. Sunderland MA: Sinauer Associates, 1988.

Luthin, Herbert W., ed. *Surviving through the Days: Translations of Native California Stories and Songs*. Berkeley CA: University of California Press, 2002.

MacAdams, Lewis. *The River: Books One, Two, and Three*. Santa Cruz CA: Blue Press, 2005.

Madigan, Nick. "Sacred Lands." *Daily Breeze*, November 27, 1993, D1.

———. "Developer Unearths Burial Ground and Stirs Up Anger among Indians." *New York Times*, January 2, 2004, A14.

Man, Coyote. *Sun Moon and Stars*. Berkeley CA: Brother William Press, 1973.

Margolin, Malcolm. *The Way We Lived: California Indian Reminiscences, Stories and Songs*. Berkeley CA: Heyday Books, 1981.

Mason, William. "Indian-Mexican Cultural Exchange in the Los Angeles Area, 1781–1834." *Aztlan* 15, no. 1 (1984): 123–45.

Mathez, Edmond A. "Introduction." *Earth: Inside and Out*, edited by E. A. Mathez. New York: New Press, 2001.

Mayewski, Paul A. "An Ice Core Time Machine." In *Earth: Inside and Out*, edited by E. A. Mathez. New York: New Press, 2001.

McCall, Lynn, and Rosalind Perry, eds. *California's Chumash Indians*. San Luis Obispo CA: EZ Nature Books, 1996.

McCawley, William. Interview by author. Santa Monica CA, July 1992; June 1993.

———. *The First Angelinos: The Gabrielino Indians of Los Angeles*. Banning CA: Malki Museum Press, 1996.

McGowan, Charlotte. *Ceremonial Fertility Sites in*

Southern California. San Diego Museum Papers 14. San Diego CA: San Diego Museum of Man, 1982.

McInnis, Douglas. "Vanished: Who Pulled the Plug on the Mediterranean? And Could It Happen Again?" *New Scientist* 2198 (August 7, 1999).

McKenzie, Dan. "Seafloor Magnetism and Drifting Continents." In *A Century of Nature: 21 Discoveries That Changed Science and the World*, edited by Laura Garwin and Tim Lincoln, 131–37. Chicago: University of Chicago Press, 2003.

McLellan, Bryan. "An Island of History." *Outlook Mail*, September 14, 1994, A1.

McPhee, John. *The Control of Nature.* New York: Noonday Press, 1989.

———. *Assembling California.* New York: Farrar, Straus & Giroux, 1993.

McWilliams, Carey. *Southern California: An Island on the Land.* Salt Lake City: Peregrine Smith Books, 1946.

Meighan, Clement W. Letter to W. E. Dean. Malibu CA, September 29, 1952.

———. Interview by author. Santa Monica CA, August 15, 1986.

Merriam, C. Hart. *Studies of California Indians.* Berkeley CA: University of California Press, 1955.

Miller, Bruce W. *The Gabrielino.* Los Osos CA: Sand River Press, 1991.

Mojzsis, Stephen J. "Life and the Evolution of Earth's Atmosphere." In *Earth: Inside and Out*, edited by E. A. Mathez. New York: New Press, 2001.

Monastero, F. C., A. E. Sabin, and J. D. Walker. "Evidence for Post–Early Miocene Initiation of Movement on the Garlock Fault from Offset of the Cudahy Camp Formation, East-Central California." *Geology* 25, no. 3 (March 1997): 247–50.

Moores, E. M. "Southwest U.S.–East Antarctic (SWEAT) Connection: A Hypothesis." *Geology* 19 (1991): 425–28.

Moriarty, James Robert. *Chinigchinix: An Indigenous California Indian Religion.* Los Angeles: Southwest Museum, 1969.

Morrison, Patt. *Rio L.A.: Tales from the Los Angeles River.* Santa Monica CA: Angel City Press, 2001.

Myerhoff, Barbara G. "The Doctor as Culture Hero: The Shaman of Rincon." *Anthropological Quarterly* 39 (1966): 60–72.

Nabokov, Peter. "City Is Losing a Part of Its Soul in Playa Vista." *Los Angeles Times*, June 7, 2004, B9.

———. *Where the Lightning Strikes: The Lives of American Indian Sacred Places.* New York: Penguin Books, 2006.

National Parks Service. *The Native Americans of Joshua Tree National Park: An Ethnographic Overview and Assessment Study.* By Cultural Systems Research, Inc. August 22, 2002 (updated August 4, 2004). http://www.nps.gov/history/history/online_books/jotr/history1.htm.

Oakeshott, Gordon B. 1978. *California's Changing Landscapes: A Guide to the Geology of the State.* New York: McGraw-Hill.

O'Lague, Paul. Interview by author. Santa Monica CA, March 2002; May 2003; September 2008.

Oak Ridge National Laboratory. "North America during the Last 150,000 Years." Compiled by Jonathan Adams, Environmental Sciences Division. http://www.esd.ornl.gov/projects/qen/nercNORTHAMERICA.html.

Oxburgh, Rachel. "Earth: The Goldilocks Planet." In *Earth: Inside and Out*, edited by E. A. Mathez. New York: New Press, 2001.

Padmanabhan, T. *After the First Three Minutes: The Story of Our Universe.* Cambridge: Cambridge University Press, 1998.

Patencio, Chief Francisco. *Stories and Legends of the Palm Springs Indians as told to Margaret Boynton.* Los Angeles: Times Mirror, 1943.

———. *Desert Hours with Chief Patencio as told to Kate Collins.* Palm Springs CA: Palm Springs Desert Museum, 1971.

Pendell, Dale. *Pharmako/Gnosis: Plant Teachers and the Poison Path.* San Francisco: Mercury House, 2005.

Perkins, Sid. "Subway Dig in L.A. Yields Fossil Trove." *Science News*, December 23, 30, 2000, 416.

———. "Northern Extinction: Alaskan Horses Shrank, Then Disappeared." *Science News*, November 15, 2003, 307–8.

Perry, Jennifer E. "Chumash Ritual and Sacred Geography on Santa Cruz Island, California." *Journal of California and Great Basin Anthropology* 27, no. 2 (2007): 103–24.

Peterson, G. L., R. G. Gastil, and E. C. Allison. "Geology of the Peninsular Ranges." California Division of Mines and Geology: Mineral and Water Resources of California, Bulletin 191, 1966.

Phillips, Tony. "Earth's Inconstant Magnetic Field." *Science @ NASA*, December 29, 2003. http://science.nasa.gov/headlines/Y2003/29dec_magneticfield.htm

Pitt, Leonard. *The Decline of the Californios: A Social History of the Spanish-Speaking Californians, 1846–1890.* Berkeley CA: University of California Press, 1971.

Pitt, Leonard, and Dale Pitt. *Los Angeles A to Z: An Encyclopedia of the City and County.* Berkeley CA: University of California Press, 1997.

Palakovic, Gary. "Channel Island Woman's Bones May Rewrite History." *Los Angeles Times,* April 11, 1999, A1.

Preble, Donna. *Yamino Kwiti: A Story of Indian Life in the Los Angeles Area.* Berkeley CA: Heyday Books, 1940.

Quinn, James P. "Rancho La Brea: Geologic Setting, Late Quaternary Depositional Patterns and Mode of Fossil Accumulation." In *The Regressive Pleistocene Shoreline: Coastal Southern California.* Annual Field Trip Guide Book No. 20, South Coast Geological Society, 1992.

————. "The Geologic Setting of Rancho La Brea." *Terra* (Natural History Museum of Los Angeles County) 38, no. 2 (2001): 46–49.

Rayl, A. J. S. "Becoming a Full-Fledged Condor." *Smithsonian,* (September 2004): 92–97.

Reid, Hugo. *The Indians of Los Angeles County: Hugo Reid's Letters of 1852.* Southwest Museum Paper 21, edited by R. Heizer. Los Angeles: Southwest Museum, 1968.

Reyes, David. "Treasure Trove of Fossils Discovered in Irvine." *Los Angeles Times*, July 12, 1997, A18.

Reynolds, Richard L. "Domestic Dog Associated with Human Remains at Rancho La Brea." *Bulletin of the Southern California Academy of Sciences* 84, no. 2 (1985): 76–85.

Riney, Brad. "Plate Tectonics: How Baja California and the Sea of Cortés Were Formed." *Ocean Oasis Field Guide.* San Diego Natural History Museum (2000). http://www.oceanoasis.org/fieldguide/geology1.html

Roberts, Helen H. *Form in Primitive Music: An Analytical and Comparative Study of the Melodic Form of Some Ancient Southern California Indian Songs.* New York: W. W. Norton, 1933.

Robinson, John W. *The San Bernardinos: The Mountain Country from Cajon Pass to Oak Glen, Two Centuries of Changing Use.* Arcadia CA: Big Santa Anita Historical Society, 1989.

Rocha, Vera. Interview by author. Santa Monica CA, September 21, 1986; October 15, 1992; April 24, 1993.

Romani, John F. "Astronomy and Social Integration: An Examination of Astronomy in a Hunter and Gatherer Society." Master's thesis, California State University, Northridge, 1981.

Romani, John, Gwendolyn Romani, and Dan Larson. "Astronomical Investigations at Burro Flats: Aspects of Ceremonialism at a Chumash Rock Art and Habitation Site." In *Earth and Sky: Papers from the Northridge Conference on Archeoastronomy,* edited by A. Benson and T. Hoskinson. Thousand Oaks CA: Slo'w Press, 1985.

Romero, Jose Carlos. "Recommendations Concerning Tentative Tract No. 51122 (includes Environmental Review SEIR 91–0675)." In *Los Angeles City Planning Department Staff Report to the City Planning Commission.* Los Angeles, 1999.

Rozaire, Charles. Interview by author. Santa Monica CA, August 4, 1986.

Rozaire, Charles E., and Russel E. Belous. *Preliminary Report on the Archaeology of the La Ballona Creek Area, Los Angeles County, California.* EIR LAN-751. Los Angeles, 1950.

Santa Barbara Museum of Natural History. *California's Chumash Indians.* San Luis Obispo CA: EZ Nature Books, 1996. First published 1986 by John Daniel.

Schaffer, Jeffrey P. "California's Geological History and Changing Landscapes." In *The Jepson Manual: Higher Plants of California,* edited by J. C. Hickman. Berkeley CA: University of California Press, 1993.

Schoenherr, Allan A. *A Natural History of California.* California Natural History Guides 56, edited by A. C. Smith. Berkeley CA: University of California Press, 1992.

Seiler, Hansjakob. *Cahuilla Texts with an Introduction.* Language Science Monographs 6. Bloomington IN: Indiana University, 1970.

Selby, William A. *Rediscovering the Golden State: California Geography.* 2nd ed. Hoboken NJ: John Wiley & Sons, 2006.

Sereno, Paul C. "Dinosaurs and Drifting Continents." *Natural History* (January 1995): 40–47.

Sharp, Robert P., and Allen F. Glazner. *Geology Underfoot in Southern California.* Missoula MT: Mountain Press Publishing, 1993.

Shaw, Christopher A., and James P. Quinn. "Rancho La Brea: A Look at Coastal Southern California's Past." *California Geology* (June 1986): 123–32.

Shipek, Florence C. "History of Southern California Mission Indians." In *Handbook of North American Indians, Vol. 8: California,* edited by Robert F. Heizer, 610–18. Washington DC: Smithsonian Institution, 1978.

Simi Valley: A Journey Through Time. Simi Valley Historical Society and Museum, 1997.

Singer, Clay. Interview by author. Santa Monica CA, June 9, 1986.

Siva, Ernest H. *Voices of the Flute: Songs of Three*

Southern California Indian Nations. Banning CA: Ushkana Press, 2004.

Smith, Gerald A., Michael K. Lerch, and Harley Garbani. *Indian Pit and Petroglyphs Cuplues of Western Riverside County*. San Jacinto CA: San Jacinto Valley Museum Association and Inland Empire Museum Association, 1990.

Snyder, Gary. *The Practice of the Wild*. San Francisco: North Point Press, 1990.

Sparkman, Philip Stedman. "The Culture of the Luiseño Indians." *University of California Publications in American Archaeology and Ethnology* 8, no. 4 (August 7, 1908): 187–234; reprinted, New York: Kraus Reprint Corp., 1964.

Staedter, Tracy. "Snowball Earth Theory Comes under Fire." *Scientific American*, September 30, 2005, http://www.scientificamerican.com/article.cfm?id=snowball-earth-theory-com.

Starr, Kevin. *California: A History*. New York: Modern Library, 2005.

Stone, Richard. "Late Date for Siberian Site Challenges Bering Pathway." *Science* (July 25, 2003): 450–51.

Strong, William Duncan. *Aboriginal Society in Southern California*. Classics in California Anthropology 2. Banning CA: Malki Museum Press, 1987.

Swann, Brian, ed. *Coming to Light: Contemporary Translations of the Native Literatures of North America*. New York: Vintage Books, 1994.

———. ed. *Native American Songs and Poems: An Anthology*. Mineola NY: Dover Publications, 1996.

———. ed. *Voices from Four Directions: Contemporary Translations of the Native Literatures of North America*. Lincoln NE: University of Nebraska Press, 2004.

Swimme, Brian, and Thomas Berry. *The Universe Story: From the Primordial Flaring Forth to the Ecozoic Era, a Celebration of the Unfolding Cosmos*. San Francisco: Harper San Francisco, 1992.

Tedlock, Dennis and Jerome Rothenberg, eds. *Alcheringa: Ehnopoetics* 1, nos. 1 & 2 (1975).

Temple, Thomas Workman, II. "Toypurina the Witch and the Indian Uprising at San Gabriel." *The Masterkey for Indian Lore and History* 31, no. 6 (1957): 136–52.

Tiffney, Bruce H. Inteview by author. Santa Barbara CA, April 10, 1998.

Timbrook, Jan. *Chumash Ethnobotany: Plant Knowledge Among the Chumash People of Southern California*. Santa Barbara CA: Santa Barbara Museum of Natural History: Heyday Books, 2007.

University of California, Santa Barbara. "Tiny Diamonds on Santa Rosa Island Give Evidence of Cosmic Impact." Press release, July 21, 2009.

U.S. Army Engineer District, Los Angeles. *Los Angeles-Long Beach Harbor Areas Prehistory and Early History*. By Gary E. Stickel, 1978.

U.S. Congress Committee on Interior and Insular Affairs. *Mineral and Water Resources of California*. Committee Print. 89th Cong., 2d sess., 1966.

U.S. Geological Survey. "San Gabriel Fault." *San Andreas Fault System in the Inland Empire and Salton Trough*. http://geomaps.wr.usgs.gov/socal/geology/inland_empire/ie_san_gabriel_fault.html.

U.S. Geological Survey. *The San Andreas Fault*. http://pubs.usgs.gov/gip/earthq3/contents.html.

U.S. Geological Survey Volcano Hazards Program: Long Valley Observatory. *Photo Gallery of the Long Valley Area, California*. http://lvo.wr.usgs.gov/gallery/index.html.

Van Tilburg, Jo Anne, ed. *Ancient Images on Stone: Rock Art of the Californias*. Los Angeles: The Institute of Archaeology at UCLA, 1983.

Vane, Sylvia Brakke, and Lowell J. Bean. *California Indians: A Guide to Manuscripts, Artifacts, Documents, Serials, Music, and Illustrations*. Menlo Park CA: Ballena Press, 1990.

Walker, Phillip L., and Travis Hudson. *Chumash Healing: Changing Health and Medical Practices in an American Indian Society*. Banning CA: Malki Museum Press, 1993.

Wallace, William. Interview by author. Santa Monica CA, July 25, 1986.

———. "A Remarkable Group of Carved Stone Objects From Pacific Palisades." *Pacific Coast Archaeological Society Quarterly* 23, no.1 (1987): 47–57.

———. "Music and Musical Instruments." In *Handbook of North American Indians, Vol. 8: California*, edited by Robert F. Heizer, 642–48. Washington DC: Smithsonian Institution, 1978.

Warren, Charles S. *History of the Santa Monica Bay Region*. Santa Monica CA: A. H. Cawston, 1934.

Weaver, John D. *El Pueblo Grande: A Nonfiction Book About Los Angeles*. Los Angeles: Ward Ritchie Press, 1973.

Weber, David J. "Arts and Architecture, Force and Fear: The Spanish-Indian Struggle for Sacred Space." In *The Art of the Missions of Northern New Spain*, edited by Clara Bargellini and Michael Komanecky. Mexico City: Antiguo Colegio de San Ildefonso, 2009. (Exhibition catalog.)

Weigand, Peter W. "Geologic History of the Santa Monica Mountains: Rocks, Structures, and Tectonics." Paper read at Teacher Training Workshop, May 19–20, 1995, Northridge CA.

———. Interview by author. Northridge CA, April 1998; August 2002; September 2002.

Weigand, Peter W., and Karen L. Savage. "To Plates' Edge: Field Guide to the Geology Between the San Fernando Valley and Palmdale." Handout for A Day in the Field with Tom Dibblee, April 7, 2001. Published by Santa Barbara CA: Thomas W. Dibblee, Jr. Geological Foundation.

Weschler, Lawrence. "L.A. Glows: Why Southern California Doesn't Look Like Any Place Else." *New Yorker*, February 23, March 2, 1998, 90–97.

Whistler, David P. "Red Rock Canyon: A Geologist's Classroom." *Terra* (Natural History Museum of Los Angeles County) 21, no. 2 (1982): 3–9.

———. Interview by author. Los Angeles, March 6, 1998.

Whistler, Kenneth W. *An Interim Barbareno Chumash Dictionary (of Barbareno as Spoken by Mary Yee).* Washington DC: Smithsonian Institution, 1980.

White, Raymond C. "The Luiseño Theory of 'Knowledge.'" *American Anthropologist* 59, no. 1 (February 1957): 1–19.

———. "Luiseño Social Organization." *University of California Publications in American Archaeology and Ethnology* 48, no. 2 (1963): 91–194.

———. "Religion and Its Role among the Luiseño." In *Native Californians: A Theoretical Perspective*, edited by Lowell John Bean and Thomas C. Blackburn, 355–77. Menlo Park CA: Ballena Press, 1976.

Whitley, David S. "Shamanism and Rock Art in Far Western North America." *Cambridge Archaeological Journal* 2, no. 1 (1992): 89–113.

———. "Shamanism, Natural Modeling, and the Rock Art of Far Western North American Hunter-Gatherers." In *Shamanism and North American Rock Art*, edited by S. Turpin. San Antonio TX: Rock Art Foundation, 1998.

———. *The Art of the Shaman: Rock Art of California.* Salt Lake City: University of Utah Press, 2000.

Whitley, David S., and Ronald I. Dorn. "New Perspectives on the Clovis Vs. Pre-Clovis Controversy." *American Antiquity* 58, no. 4 (1993): 626–47.

Wilken, Dieter H. "California's Changing Climates and Flora." In *The Jepson Manual: Higher Plants of California*, edited by J. C. Hickman. Berkeley CA: University of California Press, 1993.

Williams, Walter L. *The Spirit and the Flesh: Sexual Diversity in American Indian Culture.* Boston: Beacon Press, 1992.

Woodford, A. O., J. E. Schoellhamer, J. G. Vedder, and

R. F. Yerkes. "Geology of the Los Angeles Basin." In *Geology of Southern California*, edited by R. H. Jahns. San Francisco: California Department of Natural Resources, Division of Mines, 1954.

Wylde, Hildegarde Howard. *Leisure World History.* Laguna Hills CA: Leisure World Historical Society, 1980.

Yeats, Robert S. "Rifting and Rafting in the Southern California Borderland." In *Proceedings of Conference on Geologic Problems of the San Andreas Fault System*, 307–22. Palo Alto CA: Stanford University Publications in the Geologic Sciences, 1968.

———. "Tectonics of the San Gabriel Basin and Surroundings, Southern California." *Geological Society of America Bulletin* 116 (September–October 2004): 1158–82.

Yerkes, R. F., T. H. McColloh, J. E. Schoellhamer, and J. G. Vedder. *Geology of the Los Angeles Basin California—an Introduction.* Geological Survey Professional Paper 420-A. Washington DC: United States Government Printing Office, 1965.

Young, Betty Lou, and Randy Young. *Santa Monica Canyon: A Walk through History.* Pacific Palisades CA: Casa Vieja Press, 1997.

Zhuravlev, Andrey Yu. "Reef Ecosytem Recovery after the Early Cambrian Extinction." *Geological Society, London, Special Publications* 102 (1996): 79–96.